OPPOSING VIEWPOINTS® SERIES

Africa

Other Books of Related Interest:

Opposing Viewpoints Series

AIDS

America's Global Influence

Poverty

Current Controversies Series

Developing Nations

Globalization

At Issue Series

Pandemics

Sexually Transmitted Diseases

"Congress shall make no law . . . abridging the freedom of speech, or of the press."

First Amendment to the U.S. Constitution

The basic foundation of our democracy is the First Amendment guarantee of freedom of expression. The Opposing Viewpoints Series is dedicated to the concept of this basic freedom and the idea that it is more important to practice it than to enshrine it.

OPPOSING VIEWPOINTS® SERIES

Africa

David M. Haugen, Book Editor

GREENHAVEN PRESS
A part of Gale, Cengage Learning

GALE
CENGAGE Learning™

Detroit • New York • San Francisco • New Haven, Conn • Waterville, Maine • London

GALE
CENGAGE Learning

Christine Nasso, *Publisher*
Elizabeth Des Chenes, *Managing Editor*

© 2008 Greenhaven Press, a part of Gale, Cengage Learning.

Gale and Greenhaven Press are registered trademarks used herein under license.

For more information, contact:
Greenhaven Press
27500 Drake Rd.
Farmington Hills, MI 48331-3535
Or you can visit our Internet site at gale.cengage.com

Articles in Greenhaven Press anthologies are often edited for length to meet page requirements. In addition, original titles of these works are changed to clearly present the main thesis and to explicitly indicate the author's opinion. Every effort is made to ensure that Greenhaven Press accurately reflects the original intent of the authors. Every effort has been made to trace the owners of copyrighted material.

Cover photograph reproduced by permission of © 2007 Jupiterimages Corporation.

LIBRARY OF CONGRESS CATALOGING-IN-PUBLICATION DATA

Africa / David M. Haugen, book editor.
    p. cm. -- (Opposing viewpoints)
    Includes bibliographical references and index.
    ISBN-13: 978-0-7377-3988-6 (hardcover)
    ISBN-13: 978-0-7377-3989-3 (pbk.)
    1. Africa--Social conditions--21st century. 2. Africa--Economic conditions--21st century. 3. Africa--Politics and government--21st century. I. Haugen, David M., 1969-
    HN777.A327 2008
    306.096'0905--dc22
                                                                    2008000811

Printed in the United States of America
1 2 3 4 5 6 7 12 11 10 09 08

Contents

Chapter 3: What Is the State of Democracy and Human Rights in Africa?

Chapter 4: How Can the West Help Bring Peace to Africa?

Why Consider Opposing Viewpoints?

> *"The only way in which a human being can make some approach to knowing the whole of a subject is by hearing what can be said about it by persons of every variety of opinion and studying all modes in which it can be looked at by every character of mind. No wise man ever acquired his wisdom in any mode but this."*
>
> *John Stuart Mill*

In our media-intensive culture it is not difficult to find differing opinions. Thousands of newspapers and magazines and dozens of radio and television talk shows resound with differing points of view. The difficulty lies in deciding which opinion to agree with and which "experts" seem the most credible. The more inundated we become with differing opinions and claims, the more essential it is to hone critical reading and thinking skills to evaluate these ideas. Opposing Viewpoints books address this problem directly by presenting stimulating debates that can be used to enhance and teach these skills. The varied opinions contained in each book examine many different aspects of a single issue. While examining these conveniently edited opposing views, readers can develop critical thinking skills such as the ability to compare and contrast authors' credibility, facts, argumentation styles, use of persuasive techniques, and other stylistic tools. In short, the Opposing Viewpoints Series is an ideal way to attain the higher-level thinking and reading skills so essential in a culture of diverse and contradictory opinions.

In addition to providing a tool for critical thinking, Opposing Viewpoints books challenge readers to question their own strongly held opinions and assumptions. Most people form their opinions on the basis of upbringing, peer pressure, and personal, cultural, or professional bias. By reading carefully balanced opposing views, readers must directly confront new ideas as well as the opinions of those with whom they disagree. This is not to simplistically argue that everyone who reads opposing views will—or should—change his or her opinion. Instead, the series enhances readers' understanding of their own views by encouraging confrontation with opposing ideas. Careful examination of others' views can lead to the readers' understanding of the logical inconsistencies in their own opinions, perspective on why they hold an opinion, and the consideration of the possibility that their opinion requires further evaluation.

Evaluating Other Opinions

To ensure that this type of examination occurs, Opposing Viewpoints books present all types of opinions. Prominent spokespeople on different sides of each issue as well as well-known professionals from many disciplines challenge the reader. An additional goal of the series is to provide a forum for other, less known, or even unpopular viewpoints. The opinion of an ordinary person who has had to make the decision to cut off life support from a terminally ill relative, for example, may be just as valuable and provide just as much insight as a medical ethicist's professional opinion. The editors have two additional purposes in including these less known views. One, the editors encourage readers to respect others' opinions—even when not enhanced by professional credibility. It is only by reading or listening to and objectively evaluating others' ideas that one can determine whether they are worthy of consideration. Two, the inclusion of such viewpoints encourages the important critical thinking skill of objectively evaluating an author's credentials and bias. This evaluation will illuminate an author's reasons for taking a particular stance on an issue and will aid in readers' evaluation of the author's ideas.

It is our hope that these books will give readers a deeper understanding of the issues debated and an appreciation of the complexity of even seemingly simple issues when good and honest people disagree. This awareness is particularly important in a democratic society such as ours in which people enter into public debate to determine the common good. Those with whom one disagrees should not be regarded as enemies but rather as people whose views deserve careful examination and may shed light on one's own.

Thomas Jefferson once said that "difference of opinion leads to inquiry, and inquiry to truth." Jefferson, a broadly educated man, argued that "if a nation expects to be ignorant and free . . . it expects what never was and never will be." As individuals and as a nation, it is imperative that we consider the opinions of others and examine them with skill and discernment. The Opposing Viewpoints Series is intended to help readers achieve this goal.

David L. Bender and Bruno Leone,
Founders

Introduction

"In my opinion, the problem [that explains Africa's slow development] is the system put in place during our period of colonisation. Africa is the victim and not the guilty party. Our continent has suffered because of its huge mineral resources. The colonialists made sure they kept Africans in the dark and shut their eyes while they plundered, with impunity, our wealth. . . . We are [still] being prevented from achieving our aims because of foreign meddling and interference in our African affairs."

Teodoro Obiang Nguema Mbasogo, president of Equatorial Guinea

"Power relations between Africa and the developed world can no longer simply be understood as top-down impositions from "the West." Rather, African elites are themselves agents in—and arguably major causes of—the continent's demise."

Ian Taylor, professor of international relations at the University of St. Andrews, Scotland

Africa is a continent of contrasts and diversity. Cut nearly in half by the equator, the land is separated into arid desert lands in the north and lush landscapes in the south that range from jungle to savanna. Northern nations such as Egypt, Libya, Morocco, and Tunisia are dominated by Arab peoples who, in the seventh century, migrated westward along the Mediterranean Sea. These traders and settlers rarely ventured southward across the Sahara Desert, a forbidding barrier that stretches from the Red Sea in the east to the Atlantic in the west. The southern region of the continent—known geographically as sub-Saharan Africa—is populated mainly by black Africans who are descendents of indigenous tribes that date back thousands of years. The southern tribes were and remain as diverse as the lands they settled. Divided into around one thousand ethnic groups, the black Africans formed communities that focused on a variety of livelihoods—from raising livestock in the eastern plains to hunting and gathering in the Central African rainforests. Many sub-Saharan Africans have always been engaged in some form of agriculture, but even today there exist nomadic tribes that have not shared the majority's reliance on settled subsistence farming.

While North Africa experienced growth through close contact with Europeans and Arab travelers over a period of twelve hundred years, sub-Saharan Africa developed in relative isolation until the nineteenth century when the imperialist dreams of European powers included carving up all of Africa to gain land and resources. The era of colonialism brought Christianity to Africa, but it did not bring better economic opportunities or increased standards of living that contact with the West might have brought. Many black Africans were forced into some form of slavery, working cash crops for export or toiling in mines to unearth diamonds, copper, and other mineral commodities for European markets. Focusing mainly on stripping the land of its wealth, the Europeans did not set up industry that catered to local economies. And because the white power structure was based on black servitude, there were few attempts to foster Western education upon the black subjects. This abject state of affairs lasted for roughly seventy-five years, and the legacy of colonialism contributed greatly to the problems that beset sub-Saharan Africa as it struggled for independence in the mid-twentieth century.

Sub-Saharan Africa is still at the forefront of media and popular conceptions of Africa. When the continent is mentioned in the news or even in casual conversation, the most common image in Western minds is that of impoverished black Africa. This is primarily because the more sensational news items of recent decades have involved civil wars, famines and droughts, extreme deprivation, and the AIDS crisis—all of which have plagued sub-Saharan nations. To some degree, the prevalence of these problems, coupled with a number of despotic or unstable governments, has led many to believe that Africa—meaning black Africa—is making no progress in forming a civil society that can provide for its people without charity from abroad. In a 1997 *Good News* magazine article, Melvin Rhodes, a pastor of the United Church of God in Michigan, observed, "In the three or four decades after decolonization, Africa has been the only continent that has gone backward economically. Most people today are worse off than under colonial rule."

In the decade since Rhodes's assertion, other writers—including African writers—have echoed that unusual sentiment. In a 2007 article for the African Path Web site, Dennis Matanda, a student of international relations and a commentator on Ugandan politics, blames the continent's miseries on the leaders who should be able to turn the "secret of Western society success" to Africa's advantage. Unfortunately, he argues, Africans have let themselves be ruled poorly, grumbled about political change without effecting it, and sought their salvation through outside agencies. Matanda states, "Africans and many black people all over the world are living lives below their colleagues on the opposite end of the colour spectrum. And instead of rolling up our sleeves to work on the core and source of this misery, we seem to be more obsessed with fighting for rights we do not deserve or cannot sustain."

To rectify the situation and counter the apathy of African people, Matanda recommends reinstituting Western colonialism. He writes, "Instead of wasting our time and wringing our hands in helplessness while the rest of the world slowly but surely gets numb to our pain and leaves us behind even faster, we should let these good white folk come back to actually and effectively run our African countries and affairs."

Matanda's complaint—even if meant to be more provocative than practical—strikes at the heart of an issue that is shaping opinions about sub-Saharan Africa—the region's supposed curse of poor governance. "African leaders are solely to blame for the quagmire that the African states have descended into," he insists in a subsequent article for African Path. Other voices within Africa share this view, and foreign governments are using it as a basis to redefine the assistance they will lend to sub-Saharan nations. The U.S. government, for example, created its Millennium Challenge Corporation in 2004 to give preferential aid to poor countries that could demonstrate a commitment to cleaning up corruption and a willingness to be civically responsible. Several critics, however, suggest that aid packages with strings attached are simply a manifestation of modern colonialism.

Tunde Obadina, director of Africa Business Information Services, a financial consulting organization, wrote in a 2000 article for the charity and debate forum Africa Business Analysis,

> In a way, the whites have been returning [to the former colonies in Africa]. Some would say, they never left. Over the past two decades western governments, aid agencies and multilateral finance institutions have sent experts to African countries to help them develop. The help increasingly involved attempts to direct the political and economic development of the recipient nations.

He notes that in recent years there have been what he terms "absurd" calls in Western media for the reinstitution of benign imperialism to lift Africa out of its quagmire. As Obadina notes, one foreign commentator even suggested privatizing entire sub-Saharan countries so that Western business interests could bring African economies back on track and eliminate the corruption that able business leaders could not abide. Most Western leaders and African observers who support these notions argue that Africa is simply not ready to manage its own affairs, Obadina maintains, and that foisting the Western democratic model upon Africa is the only way to overcome the persistence of poor governance. "In effect, the aim is to do now what many feel should have been done by the colonisers before they relinquished power," Obadina concludes. "That is, teach Africans how to govern themselves."

Many commentators reiterate the belief that colonialism and neo-colonialism have both perpetuated the image of the helpless African and severely derailed Africa's progress toward development. Writing in the *Financial Gazette*, a leading southern African investment and trade magazine, Charles Mangongera boldly declares,

> It is undeniable that the continent has never recovered from the looting and plunder that it was subjected to during the colonial era. It is undeniable that the Western world continues to make conscious and deliberate efforts to exacerbate Africa's isolation in the global economy. It is true that instead of helping Africa recover from the adverse impact of their colonial domination, the Western powers have sought ways to alienate Africa in terms of development by prescribing flawed experimental economic policies that have been made a precondition for aid.

In the 2002 article, Mangongera even goes on to claim, "The civil wars and conflicts that engulf Africa today have primarily stemmed from the manipulation of people's frustrations by some unscrupulous Western powers." The reason for such manipulation, Mangongera states, is to have power over the continent and its resources by keeping it dependent. But like

Matanda, he blames African leaders for continually "harping" on the legacy of colonialism and not focusing on how poor governance is compounding colonialism's ills. Leadership and coalition, Mangongera believes, are what will move Africa forward.

Both poor governance and the enduring inheritances of colonialism are common to any discussion of sub-Saharan Africa. The viewpoints anthologized in *Opposing Viewpoints: Africa* illustrate this fact. In chapters titled What Are the Most Serious Problems Facing Africa? What Economic Policies Will Benefit Africa? What Is the State of Democracy and Human Rights in Africa? How Can the West Help Bring Peace to Africa? the authors speak of many problems and policies that are affecting Africa's development in the twenty-first century. Nearly all of these issues contain some reference either to the impact of Western involvement or the concept of "good governance." The pervasiveness of these topics suggests that they will both have to be addressed if sub-Saharan Africa is to move forward.

OPPOSING
VIEWPOINTS®
SERIES

CHAPTER 1

What Are the Most Serious Problems Facing Africa?

Chapter Preface

Few would take issue with the assertion that Africa is a continent plagued by many problems. Ethnic violence still ravages populations and displaces hundreds of thousands of refugees. Other killers such as disease, hunger, and lack of clean water claim even more lives than warfare. And the shortage of industry and job opportunities consigns vast numbers of those who survive to lives of poverty and despair. These problems are most acute in sub-Saharan Africa, where large populations coupled with lack of development have ensured low standards of living.

While the aforementioned ills of the continent have all reached the media spotlight and have been the subject of charity forums and foreign aid policies, many critics and observers suggest that famine, poverty, and other social problems are symptoms of a larger crisis in Africa—poor governance. Tunde Obadina, director of Africa Business Information Services, states plainly, "Blaming Africa's woes on bad leaders has become the mantra of many people concerned about the continent's future." He adds that there is a tendency to point the finger at "the excesses of individual dictators and their cronies." Indeed, many sub-Saharan nations have suffered under the rule of tyrants. Mobutu Sese Seko, the former ruler of the Democratic Republic of the Congo (which he named Zaire during his reign) silenced political opposition and plundered the nation's wealth during his three decades of power (1965–1997). Robert Mugabe, the current president of Zimbabwe, rose to power in 1980 and has since been blamed for the economic ruin of his nation and the mass starvation of his people while suppressing dissenters who have rejected his reform policies. Other leaders brought to power by military coups or suspect elections have reinforced this notion that government corruption is thwarting development.

Outside the continent, the view that Africa is troubled by poor governance is at the heart of foreign policy. The USAID program, which administers part of the U.S. assistance to Africa, begins its report on African governance by stating, "Weaknesses in democratic governance dampen economic activity, cause civil unrest, and can create fertile ground for terrorists." The organization cites democratic practices as a prerequisite for sustainable development, taking the view that responsible government will lead to improved education, health, and economic growth. The United States has even created a special aid program—the Millennium Challenge Account—through which more financial assistance is given to developing nations that demonstrate good governance.

Some commentators both inside and outside Africa, however, claim that the focus on poor governance—and especially on its supposed connection to terrorism—is just a means for the United States to promote its interests in reforming unfriendly governments and gaining access to African markets. Writing about how he and other Africans first came in contact with the Western notion of "good governance" at a 1991 conference of the Global Coalition for Africa, Julius Nyerere says that "the arrogant and patronising manner in which it was raised by the aid givers ... discredited the whole subject in the eyes of many of us in Africa and other parts of the South. For used in this manner, good governance sounded like a tool for neo-colonialism." And while Nyerere and others acknowledge that African governments still are in the necessary process of democratic reform, they are quick to point out that poverty, hunger, and poor health care may have as much to do with the external pressures of globalization and the contingencies of aid packages as with internal mismanagement and corruption.

In the following chapter, analysts present some of the specific problems—possibly linked to poor governance—that have stalled development of sub-Saharan Africa.

> *"While most women don't choose prostitution, many are compelled by a lack of economic, legal, and cultural power to do things that expose them to AIDS."*

AIDS Is a Serious Problem in Africa

Abraham McLaughlin

Abraham McLaughlin reports in the following viewpoint that many African women face a greater exposure to AIDS than do men. Factors such as the economy, culture, and women's rights influence the choices women make, such as prostitution, that can expose them to AIDS. Groups educating Ugandan women, with a concentration on abstinence and safe sex practices, hope to empower women to seek alternatives to prostitution. Abraham McLaughlin is a staff writer for the Christian Science Monitor.

As you read, consider the following questions:

1. How many times more likely are adult women to get AIDS than adult men in Africa?

2. In what ways are Ugandan groups trying to encourage young teens to refrain from early sexual activity?

3. According to Jauhara Naluyange, what is the biggest problem women face regarding early sexual activity and the risk of AIDS?

Jauhara Naluyange has been off the street for eight months now. Three years ago, at age 16, she left home and entered the commercial-sex trade. She wanted to be like the hip kids in school, craving their "cool clothes, cool bags, and cellphones." But she was from one of Uganda's poorest slums and could seldom afford more than porridge for lunch.

Then one day the older girls shared their secret. "During holidays we go onto the street," they said. "Come with us."

Thus began her journey down into prostitution—and up, eventually, into a new life. It was a woman with a gruff voice and a quick smile who helped her escape. Now Jauhara cuts and braids hair for a living.

African Women Facing AIDS

Jauhara's story is an extreme example of the pressures facing African girls and women today. While most women don't choose prostitution, many are compelled by a lack of economic, legal, and cultural power to do things that expose them to AIDS. And in a part of the world where a new United Nations study says young women are three times more likely to contract HIV than men their age, leveling the economic and social playing field has become the new focus in the battle against the virus that can lead to AIDS.

Past anti-AIDS efforts in Africa have centered around distributing condoms and preaching the benefits of abstinence and safe sex. But the efforts in Uganda, long a leader in AIDS prevention, highlight the current thinking on how to best tackle the epidemic:

"Boosting women's economic opportunities and social power," says the annual UN AIDS report, "should be seen as part and parcel of potentially successful and sustainable AIDS strategies."

Out of sub-Sahara's HIV-positive young people, 76 percent are female, according to the report. Africa's adult women, meanwhile, are 1.3 times more likely to get the disease than adult men. And overall, women and girls make up a disproportionate 57 percent of Africa's estimated 25.4 million people diagnosed as HIV positive.

The Need for Cultural Change

These numbers are increasingly cited as reason to change longstanding gender inequalities and cultural practices. A bill in Uganda's parliament, for instance, would address a host of customs—from polygamy to marital rape to bride price. Bride price is the widely practiced custom of men paying the wife's family before the wedding. Women's advocates say it often allows women to be treated as property. It can be used to give legitimacy, for instance, to a man forcing his wife to have sex. If a wife dies, men can argue that the money paid to the woman's family is transferable—and demand to marry her sister. Sometimes men want a refund so they can afford to marry again. All of these practices can spread AIDS.

Uganda's proposed law would make bride price optional, nontransferable, and nonrefundable.

But such practices have long been a key part of traditional societies. Salome Kimbugwe, coordinator of the Uganda Women's Network, which supports the law, recalls a discussion with a rural elder about bride price and women's property rights. The man asked: "But how can property own property? Can a table own a chair?"

Jobs Lead to Safe Sex and Abstinence

For Jauhara, it was Joyce Kintu who helped her. Ms. Kintu is known as "Mama Joyce" in Kawempe, one of Kampala's toughest slums. She runs a small community center here funded by the African Medical & Research Foundation, a nonprofit based in Nairobi, Kenya. Jauhara and about 40 other former sex

HIV and AIDS Statistics 2004 and 2006 for Sub-Saharan Africa		
	2004	**2006**
Adults and children living with HIV	23.6 million [20.9–26.4 million]	24.7 million [21.8–27.7 million]
Adults and children newly infected with HIV	2.6 million [2.2–2.9 million]	2.8 million [2.4–3.2 million]
Adult (15–49) prevalence (%)	6.0% [5.3%–6.8%]	5.9% [5.2%–6.7%]
Adult and child deaths due to AIDS	1.9 million [1.7–2.3 million]	2.1 million [1.8–2.4 million]

TAKEN FROM: UNAIDS, *AIDS Epidemic Update*, December 2006.

workers come daily to learn a new trade—hairdressing or tailoring. Kintu pays professional hairdressers to teach the women to add braids, straighten hair, and more. They can earn $5 or $7 for braiding a full head, although it can take all day. Which is exactly the point, Kintu says. "When they're working all day, they're tired at night"—too tired to walk the streets, she says.

Meanwhile, a focus on abstinence is seeing a resurgence, but this time it is tied to the efforts to empower women. A growing number of Ugandan groups—led by religious leaders and the first lady—are hoping to steer teens away from early sex. It's spawning what one local paper dubbed the "virginity craze." A recent event hosted by first lady Janet Museveni showcased 600 "virgins" who've pledged abstinence. The effort in this highly religious nation is partly a backlash against recent marketing efforts to boost condom use.

The trouble with advocating condoms more aggressively than abstinence or faithfulness is that "many people who fail to abstain eventually fail to use a condom," says Luboga Samuel, a professor at Makerere University's medical school in Kampala and chairman of the Uganda Youth Forum. The group encourages teens to take abstinence pledges, seek counseling if they're being pressured to have sex, and choose supportive friends.

Indeed, the biggest problem is "group influence," says Jauhara, who does not have AIDS, recalling how those girls in school seemed "so old and so cool."

But as she gets older—and more educated—she's gaining the confidence to stay off the street permanently. "Now that I've grown up," she says, "I won't go back."

"There has been no AIDS epidemic in Africa."

The AIDS Epidemic in Africa Is Exaggerated

Tom Bethell

Tom Bethell is a senior editor of the American Spectator *and author of* The Politically Incorrect Guide to Science *and* The Noblest Triumph: Property and Prosperity Through the Ages. *In the following viewpoint, he argues that the AIDS problem in Africa has been exaggerated. He believes reports of an AIDS epidemic on that continent have been based on erroneous measurements put forth by groups that have a political and financial interest in inflating the crisis. He asserts that if AIDS has been so devastating to Africa, then the population of the continent should have dropped significantly. But in fact, he states, African nations are still showing high population growth rates over the twenty years that AIDS has been a global concern.*

As you read, consider the following questions:

1. As Bethell states, what happened at the Bangui meeting in 1985 that has changed the way in which AIDS was reported by health organizations?

2. Why does Bethell claim that "'AIDS' in Africa has never been shown to be the same as AIDS here [in America]"?

3. What does Bethell believe is at the root of the ill health and inflated AIDS-related cases in Africa?

I was planning to wax indignant about rock stars like Bono and Bob Geldof who have been preaching in the White House about Africa's plight. What do they know? Now I am beginning to suspect they know as much as the politicians— not that that is saying much. Aid agencies are mostly interested in enlarging their own budgets. Rock musicians have other incentives, vanity admittedly among them. But they do want to see an improvement on the ground. And they have begun to address some of the more important matters, such as African rulers who steal the money and put it in Swiss banks—*bad government*, in short. Aid officials, under the thumb of the State Department and diplomatic to a fault, don't like to mention such things.

But there's something else that no one wants to mention, especially not politically progressive rock singers. In parts of tropical Africa a deterioration of the physical infrastructure swiftly followed the end of colonial rule. Sewage and sanitation crumbled. The issue is sensitive because it suggests that Africans were better off—or at least were in better health— under colonial rule. And one more thing: the unsanitary conditions were sufficient to cause "AIDS." I shall explain why.

Bad Conditions Abound

An official from the U.S. Centers for Disease Control (CDC), who was in Kinshasa, Zaire, in 1965, found it was then still "a city that worked—a marked contrast to what it's like these days. Traffic coasted down wide, well-maintained boulevards flanked by palm trees. At night the city was brilliant with light, and when you turned on the taps, water would flow out." When he returned in the 1980s he was "struck by how much the place had deteriorated."

From London's *Daily Telegraph*, July 6, 2005: On the out-skirts of African cities,

> in vast shanty towns, human beings endure privation and squalor of a kind that disappeared from the rich world generations ago. Families live in shacks fashioned from cardboard boxes and twisted metal. Fetid heaps of rubbish are everywhere, sometimes dotted with scavenging vultures. People must defecate into plastic bags, tossing the results onto piles of refuse. Naked infants have nowhere to play, save for ditches running with sewage.

From the *Daily Mail*, July 20, 2005:

> African trypanosamiasis, also known as sleeping sickness, [is] one of several horrific diseases to have made a big resurgence in south Sudan and other forgotten corners of Africa in recent years. Sleeping sickness, virtually eliminated in the 1960s, now afflicts up to 300,000 new victims in Africa each year and the figures are rising. Without treatment, the disease is fatal.

The president of the U.N. General Assembly said recently that "you can break down figures that show that 300 million people south of the Sahara don't have clean water." He described the mother with infant who lights up with a smile when offered a bottle of water, knowing that "the only alternative is to walk for two or three miles and then only to get polluted water."

Blaming Everything on AIDS

Well, we know what caused all this disease in sub-Saharan Africa, don't we, because we read about the "epidemic" almost every day in the *New York Times*. The culprit is the human immunodeficiency virus. And we know the treatment for that: nucleoside analogs, protease inhibitors, highly active antiretroviral treatment—those are the recommendations of the

AIDS activists. Let them eat retrovir, nevirapine, AZT. Oh, and don't forget to use condoms. Billions need to be shipped right away.

Africans can be forgiven for thinking that Americans believe there are too many of them. Let's hope they don't see the recent [CBS News commentator] Andy Rooney column, in which he complained: "The birthrate in Africa is a disgrace and birth control information and condoms should be handed out before the food."

Is that where liberalism is headed?

Redefining AIDS to Suit Political Aims

What about that virus and the AIDS epidemic? An epidemic is defined as a widespread outbreak of an infectious disease. And defined that way, there has been no AIDS epidemic in Africa. An epidemic of politics, yes. I have written about this before (Oct. 2003) but I have new information, so listen up.

The official who noted the deterioration in Kinshasa, Joseph B. McCormick, was responsible for organizing a meeting in Bangui, the capital of the Central African Republic. It is where Jean-Bedel Bokassa crowned himself emperor, plundered the treasury, and ate his enemies. It is "one of the most severely poverty-stricken countries on the continent," McCormick wrote.

The Bangui meeting, in October 1985, was ostensibly run by the World Health Organization [WHO] but actually set up by the CDC. At the meeting, "AIDS in Africa" was defined anew. Henceforth a combination of the following symptoms would suffice for an AIDS diagnosis: weight loss, fever, diarrhea, swollen glands, a cough, prolonged fatigue.

McCormick describes this bold act of redefinition in a book called *Level 4: Virus Hunters of the CDC* (1999). The "African AIDS" epidemic began as the meeting ended, because the unhealthy environment had already generated these symptoms in millions of Africans. No HIV test, and therefore no HIV, was needed to make the AIDS diagnosis.

You can look it up for yourself. Type "Bangui-1985 report" into Google.You will come to a WHO document: "WORK-SHOP ON AIDS IN CENTRAL AFRICA, Bangui, Central African Republic, 22 to 25 October, 1985." Page 15 "scores" the various conditions that define African AIDS: Weight loss of 10 percent and a protracted feeling of weakness (called "asthenia") get 4 points each. Repeated fever for more than a month, 3 points, repeated diarrhea, 3 points. Cough, 2; swollen glands, 2; and so on. "The diagnosis of AIDS is established when the score is 12 or more."

Sickness, caused by the prevailing unsanitary conditions, could now be called "AIDS." And that is what happened. Many deaths, the causes of which had never before been specified or even reported, were simply placed in the "HIV/AIDS" column. The 10 million orphans? An African "orphan" is someone age 15 or more with one parent "missing."

The Bangui definition established heterosexual AIDS, because the defining symptoms are found in women as often as men. McCormick went on to become assistant to the director, Division of HIV/AIDS at the CDC. And by 1993, Planned Parenthood was preaching that "sex between men and women is the most common cause of HIV infection."

False Positives in AIDS Testing

American public health officials say "no problem." Whenever an HIV test *is* administered in Africa, they say, the percentages found to be "positive" match those estimated to have AIDS by the above definition. HIV tests are administered at pre-natal clinics in South Africa, and many women are found to be "positive." What is concealed in the fine print, however, is that many conditions, including pregnancy, are sufficient to trigger a "false positive" on the HIV tests.

United Nations AIDS Agency
Overestimated Disease Statistics

Years of HIV overestimates, researchers say, flowed from the long-held assumption that the extent of infection among pregnant women who attended prenatal clinics provided a rough proxy for the rate among all working-age adults in a country. Working age was usually defined as 15 to 49. These rates also were among the only nationwide data available for many years, especially in Africa, where health tracking was generally rudimentary.

The new studies show, however, that these earlier estimates were skewed in favor of young, sexually active women in the urban areas that had prenatal clinics. Researchers now know that the HIV rate among these women tends to be higher than among the general population.

The new studies rely on random testing conducted across entire countries, rather than just among pregnant women, and they generally require two forms of blood testing to guard against the numerous false positive results that inflated early estimates of the disease.

Craig Timberg, Washington Post, *April 6, 2006.*

Abbott Laboratories, manufacturer of the main HIV test, said in 1997 that "at present there is no recognized standard for establishing the presence and absence of HIV-1 antibody in human blood." About 70 conditions have been shown to trigger a false positive, so the test is essentially useless in countries where bacterial contamination is endemic.

No Decrease in Population

Therefore "AIDS" in Africa has never been shown to be the same as AIDS here. One convincing way to demonstrate a real epidemic would be to show a sharp increase in mortality and a decline in population. Enough time has now elapsed—20 years exactly—to know that this has not happened.

The U.N. Population Division estimates that the sub-Saharan population of Africa was 434 million in 1985—the year when the "AIDS pandemic" began. Recently, the Population Reference Bureau in Washington, D.C. published its "World Population Highlights." The sub-Saharan population in 2004 was 733 million, they said. Let's say that population is the same now (no doubt it's higher). Since 1985, then, the population of sub-Saharan Africa has increased by 299 million people—a 70 percent increase. "Sub-Saharan Africa and western Asia are the fastest growing regions of the world," says the Population Reference Bureau.

For years we have been warned of the tremendous African AIDS crisis. In 2000, [Vice President] Al Gore and Madam Secretary [Madeleine] Albright took the issue to the U.N. Security Council. Laurie Garrett, who has made a career for herself predicting "plagues" that never arrive, compares it to the Black Death—in which perhaps one-third of Europe's population died in a few years.

But in sub-Saharan Africa, in 20 years, the population increased by more than the entire population of the United States (296 million today [2005]).

The sheer dishonesty of the *New York Times* and other media in not reporting these facts is hard to take. For two decades, the newspaper has campaigned against an illusory crisis. There has been no acknowledgment that public health agencies—particularly the Centers for Disease Control and the World Health Organization—have their own vested interest. The political roots of the alleged epidemic have remained concealed.

Skewed Reporting

The problem has been acute at the *Times*, both because of its national influence and because its longtime AIDS reporter,

Lawrence K. Altman, is a former employee of the CDC. (He also sits on an advisory board that administers a CDC fellowship program.) Altman graduated from the agency's Epidemic Intelligence Service in 1963 and became editor of the CDC's *Morbidity and Mortality Weekly Report.* Later he was chief of the U.S. Public Health Service's Division of Epidemiology in Washington.

Altman has been the paper's main AIDS reporter since the epidemic began. He wrote what may even have been the first article on AIDS for a national newspaper, which appeared under the politically incorrect headline, "Rare Cancer Seen in 41 Homosexuals" (*NYT,* July 3, 1981). Well, that soon changed, because heterosexual transmission was established—by redefinition in Africa.

The *Times* has systematically misreported the AIDS story since 1985. Altman's background suggests that he must have known better. In one article he mentioned the Bangui meeting, but with no details. ("They will work to create a hospital surveillance system to determine the extent of AIDS in Africa." [Nov. 8, 1985]) Over the last 20 years, the *Times* has in effect formed an unacknowledged alliance with the CDC.

A spreading infectious disease does wonders for public-health budgets. All government agencies have a vested interest in their own expansion, and all are inclined to stress the crises that will appear if their budgets are restricted. The CIA exaggerated Soviet economic strength, perhaps by a factor, often. I suppose it all depends on which agency is being gored: Pentagon, bad; Centers for Disease Control, good. Weapons, bad; pills, good.

Politicians are more easily scared into action by talk of infectious diseases than by a deteriorating public-health infrastructure—which is what really happened in sub-Saharan Africa. Politicians fear that if they do nothing about a looming epidemic, they will be blamed. In Africa, it worked. Budgetary restraint was abandoned. The Bush administration was persuaded to part with $15 billion of U.S. taxpayers' money. No one involved wanted to discuss the collapsing public-health infrastructure and its political causes.

Looking at Reliable Statistics

The South African writer Rian Malan has been a shining exception to the rule of bad reporting on African AIDS. He wrote a great article for *Rolling Stone* in 2001 (hats off to Jann Wenner, the editor). One country in sub-Saharan Africa keeps reliable vital statistics on births and deaths, Malan wrote— South Africa. But the "crisis" statistics always come from the World Health Organization in Geneva; never Pretoria. And deaths reported to Pretoria were not compatible with the very high Geneva estimates.

I checked this out in many of the dozens of the *New York Times*'s front-page stories on AIDS in Africa. They give the alleged infection rates, in which the conditions that trigger false positives are never mentioned; and the estimated AIDS deaths—from Geneva. In the end the only way to tell if there was an epidemic of the magnitude estimated is to look at the actual population figures.

In July 2000, the U.S. Census Bureau and Agency for International Development predicted negative population growth for Botswana and South Africa by 2003. But as Malan reported in the *Spectator* (UK) last October [2004]:

> When 2003 arrived both Botswana and South Africa had conducted censuses, and the results were mortifying: both countries' populations were growing fairly rapidly. In South Africa, growth came very close to the level projected with no AIDS at all—even among young adult females, who were supposedly dying like flies of HIV infection. As usual, this confounding development was ignored by the craven lickspittles of AIDS journalism.

"Most Ethiopians earn their livelihoods from agriculture, and anything that promises to increase incomes and help Ethiopia compete on the global stage is welcome."

Trying to Overcome Famine Is a Problem Facing Africa

Scott Baldauf

Scott Baldauf reports in the following viewpoint that Ethiopia is one of the largest maize producers in Africa, yet, the people in Ethiopia are starving, and only 30 percent of the food harvested reaches the market. He argues that farmers only travel about twelve miles outside their farms to sell the food they grow and have no idea how a global market actually works. If more and more Ethiopian farmers are taught and exposed to a commodity market, then they may have the ability to overcome a failing economy and pull themselves out of famine. Scott Baldauf is a staff writer for the Christian Science Monitor.

As you read, consider the following questions:

    1. What foods do Ethiopian farmers harvest?

2. Recently, Ethiopian farmers are beginning to grow profitable crops. Which crop is being produced most and is being sold in the Middle East?

3. According to the article, what is the only way in which a commodity market will work in Ethiopia?

Imagine if Ethiopia, that land of skin-and-bone children that defined African famine in the 1980s, could turn from the world's largest recipient of food aid into a bread basket, not only feeding itself, but its neighbors also.

It could happen.

Ethiopia Ending Its Own Famine

Ethiopia actually produces more maize than east African neighbors Kenya, Uganda, and Tanzania combined, but since most Ethiopian farmers are subsistence growers, only 30 percent of that food actually reaches the market.

The quickest way to change this, says economist Eleni Gabre-Madhin, is to bring profit back into agriculture, to give Ethiopian farmers enough information so that they can grow what the world wants and get paid more for growing it.

"Ethiopia is the second-largest maize producer in Africa, and yet Ethiopian farmers are getting poorer and poorer," says Ms. Gabre-Madhin, the head of Ethiopia's soon-to-be-functioning commodities exchange. "We're going to have to do something very dramatically different. The stakes are high."

What Gabre-Madhin is proposing may sound grandiose—she wants to set up a commodities exchange, similar to the Chicago Board of Trade. But her free-market passion has convinced Ethiopia's left-leaning Prime Minister Meles Zenawi to make her proposal his top domestic priority [in 2007]. Most Ethiopians earn their livelihoods from agriculture, and anything that promises to increase incomes and help Ethiopia compete on the global stage is welcome.

"You can see in the world today that globalization is a trend, and Ethiopia cannot be a country outside the global effort," says Berhan Hailu, Ethiopia's minister of information. "The government has been following the free market since 1993–94, and now the government is taking concrete means to bring this about in agriculture."

Farming in Ethiopia to Make a Profit

There are 10 million farmers in Ethiopia, a country of 80 million, growing mostly cereals such as wheat, maize, sorghum, barley, sesame, and an Ethiopian grain called "teff." Yet, few farmers travel more than 12 miles from their homes in their lifetimes, so they have very little information about what their food would be worth if they did decide to sell it. When they do sell, they sell to a local trader, who then sells to another trader, and another, adding cost to the food when it finally reaches the consumer in large cities like the capital, Addis Ababa.

"The farmer doesn't know the price—he might get five cents here, but on the other side of the country, where there's a drought, he might get three times the price," says Gabre-Madhin. "So let's imagine the farmer goes to a warehouse where you have constant updates with the latest market prices. Now the farmer starts thinking nationally, not locally."

Similarly, traders in Addis Ababa would never buy product unless they saw the quality themselves. This is understandable. Some farmers have a nasty habit of adding dust and stones to their grain to increase the weight—and, thus, the value—of each sack sold. Under Gabre-Madhin's plan, each warehouse would have an independent neutral party that would test and grade the farmer's harvest, allowing traders in Addis Ababa, and potentially outside Ethiopia, to place bids on food, sight unseen.

Convincing farmers and traders to abandon the only system they've ever known will not be easy, of course. But by making the process of buying and selling food more transparent and predictable, everyone should benefit.

Sacrificing Food for Cash Crops

Within Southern Africa—where, for example, tobacco production has expanded by 50 percent per year over the past
three years in communal, small-scale, and resettlement areas—the most desirable land is continually used for export
agriculture, and food production is sacrificed to boost agricultural production. After each year's harvest, the soil is often left unprotected, accelerating erosion. And small farmers
are pushed ever farther into marginal land. This marginalization is not trivial: it affects the African majority, who remain wage laborers and small-scale farmers without savings
or capital to devote to expansion.

Export and foreign exchange-oriented trade has con-
signed most African farmers to shrinking returns. The declining real price of all primary commodities forces many
farmers to sell what land they have to pay the debts their
crop income can no longer sustain.

Raj Patel with Alexa Delwiche, "The Profits of Famine."
Food First Backgrounder, *Fall 2002.*

"As an investor, I need stability, and only a commodity
market can offer that," says Guruprasad Rao, an agricultural
commodities broker from Dubai, on a recent trip to Addis
Ababa to buy sesame seed. "Whenever you have a lack of information, nobody knows the size of the crop. If everyone
knows the size of the crop, they can predict prices better, and
they can make better decisions."

Ways to Save Ethiopia

Already, he sees farmers switching from their traditional crops
to more profitable export crops. Over the past three years,
sesame-seed production has risen nearly 200 percent, from

199,000 tons in 2001 to 380,000 in 2005, says Mr. Rao, even though sesame seeds are not used in local Ethiopian cuisine. All of it is destined for the Middle East. A commodities exchange will only accelerate this trend, he adds.

While most academics applaud Ethiopia's embrace of the free market, some say that there are no easy fixes for a landlocked country that lacks good roads, reliable electricity, and where there is little investment in irrigation for those years when the rain clouds don't provide.

"Ethiopia suffers routine market failures, so possibly this will help," says Ross Herbert, an economic analyst at the South African Institute for International Affairs in Johannesburg. "But the bigger problem is that there is too much peasant agriculture, and too few systems to overcome the vagaries of the weather, such as irrigation and better roads, adequate supplies of fertilizer, and so on."

Rod Gravelet-Blondin, the head of the agricultural-products division at the Johannesburg Stock Exchange, cautions that a commodities market will only work if it is actually used by the majority of the farmers and traders. "It will take time, but . . . a market-based economy is a good place to start," he says. "I think Ethiopia looked at Asia and said, 'Those guys got it right, they managed to turn their economy on its head through developing their agriculture.'"

For her part, Gabre-Madhin says she considers her project "a calling."

"Can we pull this off? I believe we can," she says. "This is not just a couple of years of my life. It's a mission."

"The dearth of leaders is the cause of Africa's misery."

Lack of Leadership Is a Serious Problem in Africa

William F. Kumuyi

In the following viewpoint, William F. Kumuyi argues that one of Africa's most pressing concerns is its lack of leadership. He maintains that competent leadership would drive African nations to improve trade, development, and democracy. However, he notes that Africa has not created enough new leaders to replace the earnest reformers of past decades and thus remains limited in its progress toward these worthwhile goals. Kumuyi is the leader of the Deeper Life Bible Church and a monthly columnist for the New African *magazine.*

As you read, consider the following questions:

1. Besides leadership, what does Kumuyi say Africa is lacking?
2. What are the seven basic roles a good leader must possess in Kumuyi's view?
3. In Kumuyi's opinion, why are leaders scarce in Africa?

William F. Kumuyi, "Wanted: Leaders!" *New African*, November 2006, pp. 20–21.

The portrait of 21st century Africa is disquieting. While Europe is taming the moon and befriending Mars, Africa trudges on in poverty, disease and illiteracy. Barring the multinational and partnership business ventures, you could rely on your fingers to count the number of indigenous African organisations with one billion dollar operating capital. And, although Europe is almost breasting the tape in the IT [information technology] and space technology race, Africa seems glued to the starting block.

Yet, as I told *New African* in an interview (*NA*, Aug/Sept [2006]) tomorrow belongs to Africa. We have the resources, the brain and the brawn. Add all this to the inflow of aid from the West and we might complete in a sprint what cost others a marathon. But there is a caveat: unless we have the right leaders doing the right things we may never emerge from the cocoon of misery.

Leadership Determines Success

Leaders! Their dearth has imposed painful limitations on our collective existence. It doesn't matter what type of organisation you are in: leadership determines success. It is a critical variable in development calculus; and its dearth is the sole restrictive force that has barred Africa and its people from moving forward and upward.

Let there be competent leaders, as many as are needed, and Africa would leap from recession to recovery, from limitation to liberation, from collective doom to continuous boom. The vibrant, dynamic and servant leadership of colonial and early independence years is hardly seen these days.

Look in the socio-political arena of Africa and check on some of the people calling the shots at various leadership levels. Do they all have the sincerity, vision and savvy of [Ghanian leader Kwame] Nkrumah, the modesty, selflessness and integrity of [Julius] Nyerere, the courage and tenacity of [former South African president Nelson] Mandela, the Spartan temperance and bravery of [Nigerian leader Obafemi] Awolowo and the charm and brilliance of [Nigeria's first president Nnamdi] Azikiwe? Post-colonial Africa is awash with leaders who misruled their nations, misled their people and misused their resources.

Africa could feed and fund the world; but it has remained poor and stunted. Reason: the continent is starved of right leadership. The dearth of leaders is the cause of Africa's misery.

Leadership is influencing others to accomplish an objective. In the process, the leader keeps the various components of the organisation steady and running so that the set objectives can be achieved.

Basic Elements of Leadership

Here, stated in this simple explanation of leadership, is the basic thing that leaders are needed to do: To birth visions, take the organisation to new heights and ensure it stays alive and runs well. For Africa, (and any organisation) this translates into seven leadership roles.

- *Dream.* Leaders are needed to birth visions. Visions are dreams about desired future states, an imaginative portrait of change. Without vision, development isn't possible. For example, the people may be dissatisfied with the status quo and begin to press for novelties to turn the tide; but it takes a leader to conceive, characterise and crystallise the change so desired and then construct the mechanism for its realisation.

- *Decision.* The running of any organisation involves making appropriate decisions. While inputs may come from members, it is the leader who sets the stage, garners the inputs and decides what holds and goes. Decision-making is the most crucial aspect of leadership. If decisions are wrong, the organisation is heading for storms.

- *Direction.* A leader leads by giving others direction. Someone says a leader knows the way, shows the way and goes the way. Thus, without a leader an organisation or a people are like a ship without a compass.

- *Design.* Any organisation runs according to specific designs—operations, staffing, training, architecture, wages, and so on. The leader designs the models for all this and decides on their adoption.

- *Development.* Africa's development is slow because it lacks enough leaders who can conduct diagnostic examination of its moribund institutions and sleepy workforce, and inject them with appropriate revival measures. Without effective leadership, development isn't possible.

- *Defence.* The threat of the enemy is real. A nation needs some defence mechanism against external aggression just as an organisation needs protection from crippling effects of sabotage from rival companies. A leader is needed to arrange defence and ensure there is a safety zone from where the organisation or nation can operate.

- *Discipline.* An organisation's workforce requires both reinforcement and sanction to keep productivity high and ensure compliance to work ethics. Motivation helps to keep productivity on the up; but it is discipline that builds an organisation's reputation. Discipline and corporate control are vested in the leadership. The leader hands out the juicy carrot, but also wields the limber rod.

The foregoing are the basic roles of leaders. They all add up to this: the leader's duties are about taking the organisation somewhere and ensuring it gets there. Thus, leadership is conceptualised in terms of change and progress. You don't need leaders if you have settled on a plateau and all you want is to ensure that the clock ticks on as usual.

Leaders Are Bred Not Born

If you have come to rest and deadness, you should get a manager, an administrator, who will ensure that things are done right, including your organisation's burial. If no change is contemplated, no revolution is desired then leaders aren't needed. But if you are seeking some sort of dramatic turnaround and a break of stale record, you need someone to make it happen—a leader. Africa needs a push; hence the call for leaders.

Leaders have become so scarce because we cop out of raising them. I won't mention names; but many great past African leaders didn't leave successors. They were voices without echoes. Pick one leader among the great ones you know and see if he has left a lookalike. If African organisations and institutions would create seedbeds for leadership capacity building, we might soon stop bemoaning the dearth of people with the brain and character needed to improve our collective existence. For example, in my own organisation—a multiracial, trans-ethnic movement with about one million membership— skill-oriented leadership training is top of our operation agenda. And this has paid off. We don't have a problem of succession when a leader at any critical level leaves. We simply fill the space with someone equally competent.

For, make no mistake: human leaders aren't heavenly creatures waiting for redeployment to the Earth. They are men and women around us who have the latent capacity to move people to achieve a set goal or arrive at a pre-determined destiny. They may be hidden from view: and we may have to pray and advertise to bring them out. But they are out there! They are raw and green and might be unaware of their leader-

Africa Is Plagued with Autocrats, Not Leaders

[Zimbabwe] is a prime example of the failure of leadership in Africa. The most educated government on the continent, one that came to power 26 years ago with such hope and promise has swept the rule of law aside, corrupted the whole democratic system and deliberately and systematically destroyed a functioning and relatively efficient and competitive African economy.

This regime, led by Mr. [Robert] Mugabe who struts the AU [African Union] stage like a Pharaoh, has seen the life expectancy of its people decline by half in ten years, seen its economic output slashed by half and its exports by two thirds and reduced the value of its currency to a tiny fraction of its value.

Eddie Cross, Enough Is Enough, July 4, 2006.
http://enoughzimbabwe.org.

ship attributes. But dust and brush them up through purposeful training and send them into the trenches. You've got generals out there in front lines.

The Trait Theory

There is a theory of leadership that accounts for the raising of leaders by this method. It is called the *Trait Theory*. This theory is similar to another one known as the *Great Events Theory*. It claims the existence of innate leadership qualities, and attributes the emergence of a person as leader to some great events, which help unlock his potentials and put them into action.

John F. Kennedy provided some support for this theory. He had saved his crew from harrowing death by hungry sharks. The feat made him a hero. When asked how he did it, he replied with a shrug, "It was involuntary; they sank my boat."

The application of both theories, however, yields a misleading assumption that leaders are born, not made. Our experience and those of great leaders contradict this claim. Granted that certain leadership traits might be inborn, a lot of leadership attributes are acquired, not inherited. Courage, integrity, character, love, judgement, technical competence are just a few examples.

What Africa Needs

The most acceptable theory is named *Transformational Leadership Theory*, which holds that people can choose to become leaders, by learning about the art and science of leadership by formal and informal means. The first step in such a training process is to learn some general things about leadership, which I will outline. For easy grasp, I have used the acronym of the word "leadership" to outline some basic facts about leaders.

Love. Leaders are lovers; otherwise they risk having treacherous yes-men on board.

Envisioning. Leaders are visionary people; they like moving things forward and are not comfortable with inertia.

Attitude. Leaders have a positive attitude about their tasks, the people and life. They are incurable optimists.

Dynamism. He or she may not look like a muscle builder; but a leader isn't a weakling with a chicken's gait. He has enough brawn for the day's job.

Empowerment. Effective leaders share their influence and spread their authority down the hierarchical lines. They empower subordinates.

Resilience. Leaders aren't quitters. They may suffer a setback; but they are soon back in the trenches.

Stress Management. Leadership is stressful. But effective leaders know how to avoid burnouts.

Heroism. Leaders harbour a success mentality and inevitably become heroes because they accomplish great things.

Integrity. This relates to moral uprightness. It's the chief attribute of a leader. Without it a leader loses his worth.

Passion. This relates to strong enthusiasm. All great leaders are men who pursue their goals with passion.

Leadership isn't only about who to be; it's also about what to be. A leader is a seer, seeker, servant, strategist, shepherd, sustainer, steward and spokesman. These functional qualities speak volumes about the nature and type of leadership that Africa needs. But I reserve the details for another day.

> "While Africa has the world's lowest lev-
> els of carbon dioxide and other green-
> house gas emissions, contributing the
> least to global climate change, it has
> been forced to bear the brunt of the
> phenomenon."

Global Warming Is a Serious Problem in Africa

Tina Butler

Tina Butler is a writer based in the San Francisco Bay Area. Her work has appeared in Zoe *magazine and* African Renaissance, *a bimonthly journal based in London that covers economic development in Africa. She is also a featured writer for mongabay-.com, an environmental Web site from which the following viewpoint was taken. In this viewpoint, Butler warns that recent scientific evidence indicates that global warming is having a critical impact on Africa. According to her, the warming of the oceans around Africa is decreasing rainfall and causing droughts. In addition, Butler claims the climate changes are threatening vegetation and encouraging the spread of disease. She worries that the large, impoverished populations of Africa will be least likely to adapt to these changes and lack the resources to stem their progress.*

Tina Butler, "Africa Heats Up—Climate Change Threatens Future of the Continent," Mongabay.com, October 11, 2005. Reproduced by permission.

As you read, consider the following questions:

1. By how many degrees has the Indian Ocean warmed since 1950, according to Butler, and how is this temperature change expected to affect monsoon winds in sub-Saharan Africa?

2. In Butler's view, how is climate change affecting livestock in Africa?

3. How is climate change linked to the spread of malaria in Africa, according to Butler?

Global warming has become an increasingly pervasive topic of discussion and concern for the scientific community. From fears over oceanic inundation of low-lying island nations such as the Maldives to glacial melting in the Arctic, higher temperatures around the globe have put experts on edge about the future of the world's health and balance. Nowhere has the phenomenon become more immediate than for the African continent. A series of recent studies have revealed a sobering future for the majority of Africa, a future predicated by undeniable and significant climate change. The threat traverses all levels of the environmental, social, political and economic spheres, from heightened socio-economic disparity to dwindling fish populations, from civil strife to desperate hunger.

Altering Seasonal Patterns

One major symptom of climate change is the disruption of regular seasonal patterns over large regions of the continent. Certain areas have long suffered from heavy flooding and drought, but these phenomena seem to be on the rise in both severity and duration. In the 1970s, an extended drought in the Sahel was responsible for the deaths of 300,000 people. The Sahel is a wide section of land that stretches from the Atlantic Ocean to what is known as the Horn of Africa, encompassing Burkina Faso, Chad, Djibouti, Eritrea, Ethiopia, Mali,

Mauritania, Niger, Nigeria, Senegal, Somalia and Sudan. This region is a zone of transition between the aridity of the Sahara Desert in the north and the sub-tropical and tropical south. Previously, the tragedy in the Sahel was attributed to factors such as over-grazing and overpopulation; however, recent information is proving otherwise.

A group of researchers presented their findings on the subject at the American Geophysical Union's annual conference in May of [2005]. Generated from the analysis of 60 separate computer simulations imitating global climate, the results infer that the temperature increase in the Indian Ocean is to blame for the present drought in southern Africa. Further, higher rainfall in the Sahel appears to be linked to temperature changes in the Atlantic. The nature of the change is not as simple as a straightforward increase in temperature however.

Warming Oceans, Warming Land

Regular droughts have decimated crop yields in various parts of the continent since 1970. The scientists' models reveal consistent and marked warming of the Indian Ocean, implying persistent and increased occurrence of drought in the Horn as well as southern Africa. Results indicate that the droughts in southern Africa can be traced directly to the change in the Indian Ocean, which has warmed by one degree Celsius since 1950. The new models show that the regular monsoon winds that bring seasonal rain to sub-Saharan Africa may be 10–20% drier than in the last 50 year period. With this warming, rainy seasons are becoming markedly shorter.

In the past, the northern Atlantic has traditionally been cooler than the southern Atlantic, drawing rain-rich winds away from the Sahel. In the last 10 years of this period however, the conditions changed so that the north Atlantic was now warmer, resulting in increased rainfall in the Sahel, ending the drought in the 1990s. In essence a sea-surface temperature reversal has occurred. On dry land, the situation is similar. It has been estimated that the average surface temperature will rise between 1.4 and 5.8 degrees in the next 100 years. The greatest warming is projected to occur in the Sahel and central southern Africa.

Further evidence along this tangent has been published in [the October 2005] *Geophysical Research Letters*, only adding to a growing collection of research on how climate change may impact the continent. A new model suggests that if greenhouse gas emissions are not curbed, higher temperatures over the Sahara will result in an additional 1 to 2 millimeters of rain to fall in the Sahel by 2050 between July and September. This may not sound like much, but compared with the drought figures for the same region in the 1980s, this amount represents a 25 to 50 percent increase in rainfall.

Plants at Risk

Another indicator for the effects of climate change is vegetation. Scientists believe that a majority of current plant matter in Africa is threatened by the new variance of seasonal patterns, water supply and a general warming trend. Researchers from England's University of York speculate that an effect comparable to the most recent Ice Age and the African forest decline 2500 years ago may occur in light of the changing climatic dynamic. With the creation of climate fluctuation models, scientists have been able to determine the hypothetical impact of predicted climatic change in the responses of over 5000 native plant species. The simulations reveal results similar to other studies, namely a rise in frequency and intensity of drought in the Sahel. Actual plant migrations out of regions like the Congo rainforests were recorded by the models. Additional findings suggest the other areas that will likely feel the impact of climate change are the eastern and southwest coast regions of Africa.

Global Warming Will Evaporate Africa's Precious Water

In the drylands, water may become a critical issue. Soaring temperatures and erratic rainfall may dry up surface water. Between 75m [million] and 250m Africans, out of the 800m or so now living in sub-Saharan Africa, may be short of water. The soil will hold less moisture, bore-holes will become contaminated, and women and girls will have to walk ever greater distances to fetch water. Vegetative cover will recede. The IPCC [Intergovernmental Panel on Climate Change] guesses that 600,000 square kilometres (232,000 square miles) of cultivable land may be ruined.

"Drying Up and Flooding Out,"
Economist, *May 10, 2007.*

With a paucity of concrete data to work with, scientists used a computer program to effectively study plant response in the face of climate change. Scientists employed a technique called a genetic algorithm to fill in gaps in knowledge. Collaborating with the Nees Institute for Biodiversity of Plants and the South African National Biodiversity Institute, the York team was able to aggregate the world's largest database of Africa-wide plant distribution maps. The Annals of the Missouri Botanical Garden—the premier research institute on African botany, featured the findings in [the summer of 2005].

Exacerbating Other Problems

Participants in the study drew the shared conclusion that beyond the environment, the predicted climate change would lead to large-scale social impacts in the continent. As resources grow more scarce, tension increases proportionately. Social effects resulting from climate change are inevitably and inextricably tied to politics. The domino effect of increased hunger, subsequent environmental stress and heightened relations between people is simply another symptom of altered climate.

Hunger currently affects about half of the continent's people. Presently, various humanitarian organizations contribute six billion dollars annually to help feed the continent. Scientists anticipate even tougher times for Africa with ballooning famines, larger in both severity and duration, stemming from a higher incidence of drought. The majority of the African population relies on rain-fed crops for subsistence, making changes in their environment, especially changes in the water supply, a dire threat. Many farmers operate lacking the most basic of irrigation systems. Close to 40 percent of the GDP [gross domestic product] of African nations comes from agriculture, with 70 percent of workers employed in the industry. When the fields fail to produce, the people struggle for survival and must look elsewhere for sustenance.

Livestock is also affected by the change as animals struggle to find water and vegetation for grazing. Other threatened organisms include fish species that also provide nourishment for people. Fish populations are dropping as the air temperature rises, interfering with the production of algae, the essential link in the aquatic food web. Overfishing is another cause. There has been a 30 percent decline in fish stocks in Lake Tanganyika over the last 80 years. Fish stocks in Ghana are down by 50 percent. Only intensifying the environmental stress, fishermen are beginning to transition into farming, which in turn leads to deforestation and its associated problems, now that the source of their original livelihood is dwindling. Increased pressure has also been placed on wild game, now increasingly hunted for food.

Paying the Price

Other related problems emanating from the warming are emerging as serious threats. With the temperature increase, malaria has been on the rise throughout the continent as mosquitoes' ranges have been expanded. The disease is affecting previously safe communities and ravaging populations. One of Africa's most noted landmarks, Mount Kilimanjaro, is also showing signs of stress from climate change. Scientists predict that most of the peak's glaciers will melt by 2020. Widespread deforestation on the lower slopes of Kilimanjaro is further compounding the effects of global warming.

The greatest and saddest irony of this dark fate projected for the continent is that while Africa has the world's lowest levels of carbon dioxide and other greenhouse gas emissions, contributing the least to global climate change, it has been forced to bear the brunt of the phenomenon. Producing just over one metric ton of carbon dioxide per person a year, Africa is the least-polluting continent on Earth. In contrast, the average American generates close to 16 metric tons over the same period. This works out to a mere four percent for the entire continent, compared with the United States' 23 percent contribution. The mostly poor, developing nations that comprise the continent are the least prepared to adapt to its effects. The impact of the warming will ultimately endanger food availability and security throughout the continent. Climate change is just another problem that compounds the continent's already grave circumstance. Without serious changes, specifically the curbing of emissions in developed nations, scientists believe climate change due to global warming will continue to cripple Africa and destroy chances for progress and the alleviation of poverty and hunger.

Periodical Bibliography

The following articles have been selected to supplement the diverse views presented in this chapter.

Peter Aldhous	"The Hidden Tragedy of Africa's HIV Crisis," *New Scientist*, July 14, 2007.
America	"Hunger in Africa," September 18, 2006.
Oli Brown, Anne Hammill, and Robert McLeman	"Climate Change as the 'New' Security Threat: Implications for Africa," *International Affairs*, November 2007.
Helen Coster	"A $5 Million Carrot," *Forbes*, October 29, 2007.
William R. Easterly	"Africa's Poverty Trap," *Wall Street Journal*, March 23, 2007.
Economist	"One Challenge Down, One to Go," May 13, 2006.
Stephan Faris	"The Real Roots of Darfur," *Atlantic Monthly*, April 2007.
Esther Kaplan	"Fairy-Tale Failure," *American Prospect*, July-August 2006.
Christina Lamb	"Mugabe: Why Africa Applauds Him," *New Statesman*, August 7, 2006.
Emily Oster	"Three Things You Don't Know About AIDS in Africa," *Esquire*, December 2006.
Fred Pearce	"The Poor Will Pay for Global Warming," *New Scientist*, November 11, 2006.
Tina Rosenberg	"When a Pill Is Not Enough," *New York Times Magazine*, August 6, 2006.
Michael Specter	"The Denialists," *New Yorker*, March 12, 2007.

CHAPTER 2

What Economic Policies Will Benefit Africa?

Chapter Preface

The economies of most sub-Saharan African nations are tied to agriculture and mineral wealth. Cocoa beans and peanuts are the major cash crops in countries such as Ghana and Senegal, while copper, gold, and diamonds are found in South Africa, the Congo, Zambia, and other nations. Industry is still in its infancy in all of sub-Saharan Africa with the exception of South Africa, and oil is only an economic force in a handful of nations that stretch along the Atlantic coast from Nigeria in the north to Angola in the south. Despite these resources, the majority of Africans are subsistence farmers, eking out their daily needs and raising little income beyond that.

Some sub-Saharan African nations have seen economic growth in recent decades. The island country of Mauritius has successfully marketed seafood, tourism, information technology, and other commodities to amass a gross domestic product of $6.5 billion in 2006. As a result the per capita income of the tiny nation is over $5,000—one of the highest of the continent. At the other end of the spectrum are poor performers such as Zimbabwe. The United Nations reported that while African economies as a whole averaged a 5.7 percent growth in 2006, Zimbabwe's output fell by 4.4 percent, and the country's inflation rate—at 1,700 percent—remains the highest in the world.

While sub-Saharan Africa has seen more economic progress rather than failure in the past decades, observers are still disappointed that the region is not doing better than it is. Many attribute the slow growth to the pervasive problems of poor governance and corruption; others add civil strife and warfare as a continual disruptive force. These obstacles have made foreign investors shy away from placing their money in African enterprises. For sub-Saharan Africans, this has meant that foreign aid is the primary source of investment in the development of economy, although critics doubt that much of the aid money is reaching the people who need it. The International Monetary Fund, supported by powerhouse economies such as the United States, have tried to improve the situation by providing more aid to nations that demonstrate good governance and by advising—some say, compelling—African nations to reduce protections and open their markets to global trade. Whether these "free trade" policies have helped or hurt Africa is still a subject of debate, as some of the viewpoints in the following chapter illustrate.

Other authors in the following chapter examine the usefulness of debt relief, foreign aid, and investment in spurring economic growth in sub-Saharan Africa. The main contention in these viewpoints is whether an increase of money and capital is enough to stimulate sub-Saharan economies and raise the standard of living. For now, Western aid lenders have embraced the philosophy that more money will benefit Africa. For example, under President George W. Bush, the United States has increased funds to forty-seven African nations, and the Group of Eight (G-8)—the consortium of the world's richest nations—agreed in 2005 to cancel $40 billion in debt owed by the world's eighteen poorest nations (fourteen of which are in Africa). How well these acts will translate into economic progress on the African continent is yet to be seen, but currently the United Nations (UN) asserts that Africa is not on track to reach the Millennium Development Goal set by the UN in 2000, which is to halve the number of people living on less than $1 per day by the year 2015.

| "Development assistance based on proven technologies and directed at measurable and practical needs . . . has a distinguished record of success."

Africa Needs Foreign Aid

Jeffrey Sachs

In the following viewpoint, American economist Jeffrey Sachs bemoans the fact that U.S. aid to Africa has been undermined by popular beliefs that it is ineffective and relatively unimportant. Sachs insists that aid programs are working—improving agriculture, education, and health—and that their impact could be much greater in Africa if the U.S. government would spend more money on them. Jeffrey Sachs is the director of the Earth Institute, a global issues research center at Columbia University. He is also a special advisor to the Secretary-General of the United Nations.

As you read, consider the following questions:

1. What are the two reasons that Sachs offers to explain the U.S. government's "retreat" from providing aid to Africa?

Jeffrey Sachs, "How Aid Can Work," *New York Review of Books*, vol. 53, December 21, 2006, p. 97. Copyright © 2006 by NYREV, Inc. Reprinted with permission from the *New York Review of Books*.

2. As Sachs relates, what types of organizations are playing an important role in providing aid to Africa? And what are some of their success stories on that continent?

3. How much money does Sachs believe the United States government should invest in aid programs to Africa in order to spread "proven technologies" throughout the continent?

In a very different era, President John Kennedy declared

> to those peoples in the huts and villages across the globe struggling to break the bonds of mass misery, we pledge our best efforts to help them help themselves, for whatever period is required—not because the Communists may be doing it, not because we seek their votes, but because it is right. If a free society cannot help the many who are poor, it cannot save the few who are rich.

It is difficult to imagine President [George W.] Bush making a similar pledge today, but he is far from alone in Washington. The idea that the US should commit its best efforts to help the world's poor is an idea shared by [multibillionaires] Bill Gates, Warren Buffett, and [former president] Jimmy Carter, but it has been almost nowhere to be found in our capital. American philanthropists and nonprofit groups have stepped forward while our government has largely disappeared from the scene.

There are various reasons for this retreat. Most importantly, our policymakers in both parties simply have not attached much importance to this "soft" stuff, although their "hard" stuff is surely not working and the lack of aid is contributing to a cascade of instability and security threats in impoverished countries such as Somalia. We are spending $550 billion per year on the military, against just $4 billion for Africa. Our African aid, incredibly, is less than three days of Pentagon spending, a mere $13 per American per year, and the equivalent of just 3 cents per $100 of US national income! The neglect has been bipartisan. The [Bill] Clinton administration allowed aid to Africa to languish at less than $2 billion per year throughout the 1990s.

A second reason for the retreat is the widespread belief that aid is simply wasted, money down the rat hole. That has surely been true of some aid, such as the "reconstruction" funding for Iraq and the cold war–era payouts to thugs such as Mobutu Sese Seko of Zaire. But these notorious cases obscure the critical fact that development assistance based on proven technologies and directed at measurable and practical needs—increased food production, disease control, safe water and sanitation, schoolrooms and clinics, roads, power grids, Internet connectivity, and the like—has a distinguished record of success.

The successful record of well-targeted aid is grudgingly acknowledged even by a prominent academic critic of aid, Professor Bill Easterly. Buried in his "Bah, Humbug" attack on foreign aid, *The White Man's Burden*, Mr. Easterly allows on page 176 that

> foreign aid likely contributed to some notable successes on a global scale, such as dramatic improvement in health and education indicators in poor countries. Life expectancy in the typical poor country has risen from forty-eight years to sixty-eight years over the past four decades. Forty years ago, 131 out of every 1,000 babies born in poor countries died before reaching their first birthday. Today, 36 out of every 1,000 babies die before their first birthday.

Two hundred pages later Mr. Easterly writes that we should

> put the focus back where it belongs: get the poorest people in the world such obvious goods as the vaccines, the antibiotics, the food supplements, the improved seeds, the fertilizer, the roads, the boreholes, the water pipes, the textbooks, and the nurses. This is not making the poor dependent on

handouts; it is giving the poorest people the health, nutrition, education, and other inputs that raise the payoff to their own efforts to better their lives.

These things could indeed be done, if American officials weren't so consistently neglectful of development issues and with many too cynical to learn about the constructive uses of development assistance. They would learn that just as American subsidies of fertilizers and high-yield seed varieties for India in the late 1960s helped create a "Green Revolution" that set that vast country on a path out of famine and on to long-term development, similar support for high-yield seeds, fertilizer, and small-scale water technologies for Africa could lift that continent out of its current hunger-disease-poverty trap. They would discover that the Gates and Rockefeller Foundations have put up $150 million in the new Alliance for a Green Revolution in Africa to support the development and uptake of high-yield seed varieties there, an effort that the US government should now join and help carry out throughout sub-Saharan Africa.

They would also discover that the American Red Cross has learned—and successfully demonstrated—how to mass-distribute antimalaria bed nets to impoverished rural populations in Africa, with such success and at such low cost that the prospect of protecting all of Africa's children from that mass killer is now actually within reach. Yet they'd also learn that the Red Cross lacks the requisite funding to provide bed nets to all who need them. They would learn that a significant number of other crippling and killing diseases, including African river blindness, schistosomiasis, trauchoma, lymphatic filariasis, hookworm, ascariasis, and trichuriasis, could be brought under control for well under $2 per American citizen per year, and perhaps just $1 per American citizen!

They would note, moreover, that the number of HIV-infected Africans on donor-supported antiretroviral therapy has climbed from zero in 2000 to 800,000 at the end of 2005,

Mixing Aid and Trade

To be sure, aid by itself cannot lift a country out of poverty. Poor countries eventually need to stand on their own feet. But the idea that free trade alone can accomplish this goal also seems wrongheaded. Many of the developmental success stories over the last fifty years have involved *both* trade and aid. Burgeoning export-driven economies, after all, often need outside help to build infrastructure and improve health and education. South Korea, an example often held up by trade advocates, still received $100 per person annually in aid between 1955 and 1972 as it was boosting its exports and growing rapidly. Botswana became one of the world's fastest growing economies between 1965 and 1995 by exporting its resources, but, again, it was also receiving roughly $125 per person in aid annually. Sometimes a mix is necessary. Then again, China and India, both rapidly growing, have received little aid over the years but also have bucked free trade when it suited them. Every country is different.

Bradford Plumer, Mother Jones Online, *July 12, 2005.*
www.motherjones.com.

and likely to well over one million today [in late 2006]. They would learn that small amounts of funding to help countries send children to school have proved successful in a number of African countries, so much so that the continent-wide goal of universal attendance in primary education is utterly within reach if financial support is provided.

As chairman of the Commission on Macroeconomics and Health of the World Health Organization (2000–2001) and director of the UN Millennium Project (2002–2006), I have led efforts that have canvassed the world's leading practitioners in disease control, food production, infrastructure development, water and sanitation, Internet connectivity, and the like, to identify practical, proven, low-cost, and scalable strategies for the world's poorest people such as those mentioned above.

Such life-saving and poverty-reducing measures raise the productivity of the poor so that they can earn and invest their way out of extreme poverty, and these measures do so at an amazingly low cost. To extend these proven technologies throughout the poorest parts of Africa would require around $75 billion per year from all donors, of which the US share would be around $30 billion per year, or roughly 25 cents per every $100 of US national income.

When we overlook the success that is possible, we become our own worst enemies. We stand by as millions die each year because they are too poor to stay alive. The inattention and neglect of our policy leaders lull us to believe casually that nothing more can be done. Meanwhile we spend hundreds of billions of dollars per year on military interventions doomed to fail, overlooking the fact that a small fraction of that money, if it were directed at development approaches, could save millions of lives and set entire regions on a path of economic growth. It is no wonder that global attitudes toward America have reached the lowest ebb in history. It is time for a new approach.

| *"Foreign aid acts as a subsidy for government corruption and incompetence."*

Africa Does Not Need Foreign Aid

Andrew Mwenda

Andrew Mwenda is the political editor of the Daily Monitor, *a Ugandan newspaper, and a well-known critic of the Ugandan government as well as foreign multinational corporations in Africa. In the following viewpoint, Mwenda argues that foreign aid is harming, not helping, Africa. He insists that aid money subsidizes African governments so that they can spend their own national incomes to fund military budgets and inflated administrative organizations. Thus, in Mwenda's view, foreign aid is a disincentive to democratic and economic reform that he believes would come about if African governments were forced to solve fiscal problems internally.*

As you read, consider the following questions:

1. According to Mwenda, what percentage of its annual budget did Uganda spend on its military in 2005?
2. Why does Mwenda believe that reforming the tax code in African nations can help bring about needed change?

Andrew Mwenda, "Foreign Aid and the Weakening of Democratic Accountability in Uganda," *CATO Institute Foreign Policy Briefing*, vol. 88, July 12, 2006, pp. 2–4. Copyright © 2006 Cato Institute. All rights reserved. Reproduced by permission.

3. How would cutting off foreign aid compel African regimes to institute reform, in Mwenda's opinion?

[In 2005] British prime minister Tony Blair brought Africa's
misery to the center of world attention. Those efforts
culminated in the G8 [world's eight richest nations] summit
in Gleneagles, Scotland, and the accompanying Live 8 concerts
organized by the Irish pop star Sir Bob Geldof. However, instead of providing a new approach to Africa's state of perma-
nent crisis, Blair, his Commission for Africa (CFA), and the
G8 summit restated the conventional and failed solutions to
African poverty by endorsing increased foreign aid and the
canceling of Africa's debts.

Those initiatives suggest that the solutions to Africa's internal crisis are external. It is true that the CFA mentioned
some domestic policy and institutional problems in Africa and
suggested remedies for them. But those internal problems
were treated as secondary causes of African poverty. However,
most of Africa's problems are internal, not external, and concern domestic policies and institutions. Until those internal
problems are addressed, no amount of Western assistance will
bring Africa out of poverty. In fact, Western assistance could
postpone much-needed reforms in the way that African countries are governed.

Africa is a large and diverse continent comprising 54 countries. Each of those countries faces unique challenges that may
indeed require different policy and political interventions.
However, the current obsession with increasing aid and debt
cancellation ignores many of the difficulties that most African
countries share.

A Disincentive to Domestic Reform

First, let us examine the proposal to increase financial aid
from the West to Africa as a way of fighting poverty on the
continent. The underlying assumption of the aid lobby is that

Africa Should Put Down Its Alms Bowl

Africa has been dependent on hand-outs for its survival. African countries depend on "international donors" for vaccines, rather than produce vaccines locally for their population. Africa has the capacity to do that. Africans spend so much of their resources on buying military ware from countries outside Africa because African countries have not learn[ed] to use their own military technology; Africans rely on institutions like the IMF [International Monetary Fund] and the World Bank, in which they have very scant regulatory authority to define their economic relationship with the rest of the world. I think it is time for African countries to take a serious look at their alms bowl and recognize the shame in carrying it about.

Obi Nwakanma, Vanguard,
July 10, 2005.

governments in Africa lack the necessary resources to generate sufficient revenue to meet their public expenditure needs in areas such as health care, education, and infrastructure. Although that argument sounds convincing, it ignores the distorted fiscal priorities of African governments.

Take the example of Uganda, a country hailed by international donors, especially the World Bank and the International Monetary Fund, as an African economic success story. The country depends on foreign aid for nearly 50 percent of her budget. Foreign aid is important in Uganda because it finances free primary education, free basic health care, and infrastructure rehabilitation and maintenance. However, is it true that without foreign aid Uganda would lack revenue to meet those public expenditure needs?

Consider Uganda's taxation policy. Tax collection by the Uganda Revenue Authority [URA] amounts to about 12 percent of GDP [gross domestic product], which is below the sub-Saharan African average of 18–20 percent and well below the government's target of 24 percent. The Ministry of Finance claims that the failure to collect more taxes is due to administrative weaknesses, which is why the URA's commissioner general, Allen Kagina, believes that more government investment in the quality of human resources and computerization of tax information is needed. As the former commissioner general of the URA, Annebritt Aslund, stated, another reason for Uganda's tax shortfall is the fact that the rich and politically well connected don't pay taxes. The top individual income tax bracket in Uganda is 30 percent. That rate may encourage some individuals to avoid payment—especially given the low quality of services that Ugandans expect to receive in return. Similarly, Uganda's corporate tax, which amounts to 42.9 percent of gross profit, is quite high and may encourage tax evasion as well as discourage investment in the formal economy. Fast-growing economies tend to have a lower tax burden. Hong Kong's corporate tax, for example, amounted to only 14.3 percent of gross profits in 2005.

Where the Money Goes

Uganda's public expenditures should also be fixed. [In 2005] the government spent 11 percent of its annual budget, or US$200 million, on the military. However, about 20 percent of that amount, or US$40 million, was lost to corruption. The army payroll includes thousands of "ghost soldiers," whose salaries go straight into the pockets of the army officers. It is apparent that Uganda spends too much on the military. After all, the government had almost wiped out the rebels from the Lord's Resistance Army by 1992, when military spending was about one-fifth of the current amount. The government also spends 12.5 percent of its annual budget on public administration that is mostly political patronage. Uganda has 68 cabinet ministers, 73 presidential advisers, a stadium-sized parliament, and numerous local governments, which [from 2005 to 2006] alone increased from 56 to 80.

The Need for Better Government

Corruption in Uganda is endemic. For example, a 2004 study by Ritva Reinikka from the World Bank and Jakob Svensson from Stockholm University found that 20 percent of Uganda's total public expenditure went for education in the mid-1990s. However, only 13 percent of Uganda's sizable education budget ever reached the schools. The rest "was captured by local officials (and politicians)." Not surprisingly, a study by Uganda's own Ministry of Finance concluded that expenditure on political patronage could be cut by 50 percent and the country would get better services at a cheaper price.

Uganda does not need more foreign aid. Rather, it needs to improve its tax administration by investing in better staff and motivating them with better pay and better facilities. It needs to tackle the problem of tax evasion by the rich and well connected. Most important, the government needs to put into place incentives for people to pay taxes. Those include a substantial reduction of Uganda's tax rates, which currently punish hard work and entrepreneurship, and a dramatic improvement in the delivery of services. Taxpayers ought to receive the services they pay for, or they should be allowed to opt out and pay for service delivery by the private sector. The government also needs to replace its profligate military and public administration expenditures with prudent fiscal policy.

Aid Can Stifle Reform

Why does the government of Uganda not implement these seemingly simple and beneficial reforms? A large part of the answer lies in the incentive structure that foreign aid creates. To start with, taxation is a politically contentious issue—

people don't like to pay taxes. Why would any government antagonize key political and business allies in the name of tax collection when international donors are forever willing to pick up the bill?

Moreover, foreign aid acts as a subsidy for government corruption and incompetence. It creates disincentives to reform tax administration and to streamline public expenditure. If donors began to turn off the aid taps, the government of Uganda would likely be forced to reform its imprudent fiscal policies or stare regime collapse in the eye. When dictators in Africa have plundered their economies, they have often found themselves in fiscal crisis. Difficulties in meeting their public expenditure needs have often sparked political struggles for reform. Many of the regimes on the continent have been saved from political collapse by foreign aid. Politically, therefore, foreign aid undermines democracy and government accountability. A smart international response to Africa's problems would involve measures that induce African governments to be more fiscally responsible, not more fiscally dependent.

Between 1960 and 2003, some US$568 billion (in 2003 dollars) poured into Africa, yet the continent has been growing poorer, not richer. Many promoters of foreign aid argue that the problem is not aid itself but how the aid is used. It is important to examine the logic behind aid, however. More money may not be the best solution to poverty for the simple reason that capital is a byproduct of the development process, not its prerequisite. True, even when African politicians and bureaucrats steal much of it, aid can occasionally help. Part of it is sometimes used to build a school here, feed a hungry village there, or deliver medicines to a village full of diseased peasants. It is important to note that such aid can achieve only short-term humanitarian objectives. In the long term, aid can stifle domestic reform and, consequently, undermine the basis for long-term economic growth and prosperity.

To hold and retain power, all governments need to deliver particular benefits to specific groups, who form the basis of their political survival. Narrowly, those benefits may include paying the military and intelligence services, the civil servants, and the political hangers-on of the regime. Broadly, they include providing social services, such as education and health, and the construction and maintenance of infrastructure. All those services require money. If the source of that money is the private sector, the government is more likely to govern in a more enlightened fashion out of self-interest. The need for resources will induce the government to negotiate with local and foreign investors about policies and institutions necessary for growth and increased productivity and thus more revenue.

The problem in many African countries is that governments look for revenue not in the domestic economy but in the pockets of international donors. Rather than listen to investors and other constituencies regarding their policy and institutional needs, many governments find it easier to negotiate with international creditors for foreign aid. In that manner, foreign aid impedes the emergence of a mutually beneficial relationship between the government and the citizens. It also encourages a dependence mentality among politicians and bureaucrats, so that every time there is a fiscal shortage, they are inclined to look for aid, rather than for policies and institutions that favor economic growth. Aid thus undermines long-term growth.

> *"Aid and debt forgiveness will not pro-*
> *mote the institutional environment of*
> *economic freedom and property rights*
> *that Africa needs to grow."*

Africa Needs Investment, Not Aid

Benjamin Powell

Benjamin Powell claims in the following viewpoint that private sector investment, not international foreign aid, will boost the economies of African countries. Powell contends that foreign aid can stifle investment by allowing receiver governments to deny economic freedom in their nations. Without economic freedom, these nations are bound to remain stagnant no matter how much aid is pumped into them, Powell asserts. Powell believes that Western governments should cut aid packages and revamp trade policies to make African markets more competitive and thus attract outside investment. Benjamin Powell is a professor of economics at Suffolk University in Boston and a research fellow at the Independent Institute, a public policy research organization.

As you read, consider the following questions:

1. How much money does Powell say was "poured into Africa" between 1970 and 2000?

2. Why does Powell believe that private investment has a better chance of stimulating an economy than foreign aid?

3. What part of global trade markets does Powell think the United States and the European Union should open up to African competition?

It is widely expected that at the G8 [Group of Eight—the eight nations that account for roughly two-thirds of the global economy] meeting in July [2005] the leaders of the wealthiest countries in the world will agree to forgive $40 billion of third world debt and may also increase economic aid to Africa. [The G8 did agree to do that.] If adopted, these policies will not help poor countries develop because they fail to address Africa's underlying problems.

Tony Blair [who was Britain's Prime Minister at the time] has recently been the leading political advocate of debt forgiveness and foreign aid. He succeeded in getting the G8 finance ministers to recommend canceling the $40 billion of debt for 18 poor countries. He's also calling for a doubling of aid to Africa.

A definition of insanity is doing the same thing over and over but still expecting a different result. Foreign aid and debt forgiveness have failed to promote growth, and there is no reason to believe Blair's latest proposals will be any different.

Between 1970 and 2000 over $400 billion was poured into Africa yet little development was achieved. Money was often stolen by corrupt government officials. Even when aid actually translated into investment, the projects were often white elephants that failed to be economically viable because governments do not make decisions based on the same profit and loss expectations that investors do.

Slow Growth in Sub-Saharan Africa

Despite the recent uptick, investment in SSA [sub-Saharan Africa] measured as a share of GDP [gross domestic product] is no higher than it was in the early 1990s. Foreign direct investment in SSA, other than in oil-exporting countries and South Africa, is still low, although South Africa has become a growing source of inward investment flows to other parts of SSA, and investment from China and India is picking up. Private sector development in SSA continues to be deterred not only by the costs of doing business, which range from administrative complexities to corruption and cumbersome legal systems, but also by the expense of such critical business services as telecommunications and energy. These costs are reflected in the region's poor showing in global business surveys, such as the World Bank's investment climate indicators. However, the Bank has also found that SSA has begun to reform business regulation: two-thirds of SSA countries made at least one positive reform in 2005-06. Tanzania and Ghana ranked among the top 10 reformers in the world, and planned reforms elsewhere should further reduce business costs throughout the region.

Abdoulaye Bio-Tchané and Benedicto Vibe Christensen,
F&D: Finance and Development, *December 2006.*

There is some rationale for debt forgiveness. After all, poorly administered loans and bad advice from Western governments helped create the debt problem. However, when debt is forgiven without addressing underlying problems, new debt just replaces the old.

From 1989 to 1997, Western creditors forgave $33 billion of debt held by 41 poor countries, but during those same years, these countries borrowed an additional $41 billion. Debt was forgiven, new debt was accumulated, little growth occurred.

Economic Freedom Aids Prosperity

Africa needs investment, not aid, if it is going to grow. Private investment is naturally channeled to the most profitable projects in a market economy. Because decisions are based on expected profits and losses, investors have the right information and incentives to make the right decisions.

Africa needs to create an environment of greater economic freedom and security in property rights to attract investment. Recent research using the Fraser Institute's economic freedom index has shown that countries with more economic freedom attract more foreign investment and have higher overall levels of investment per worker.

On a scale of 1 to 10, countries scoring lower than 5 in economic freedom only generate $845 per worker of investment, and they attract only $68 of foreign investment per worker. Meanwhile countries that score higher than 7 in economic freedom generate $10,871 of investment and $3,117 in foreign investment per worker.

Countries that are more economically free also make more productive use of their investment. Recent research by Capital University economics professor Robert Lawson found that investment generates higher economic growth rates in freer countries than in less free countries. Further, he found that even in the least free countries, private investment still generates economic growth more efficiently than public investment.

Foreign Aid Can Stall Economic Growth

Unfortunately, development aid can discourage private investment by hampering the economic freedom that is necessary to attract it. Noted development economist P.T. Bauer long contended that government-to-government aid promoted statism by politicizing economic life and enlarging the relative size of the public sphere. Recent research by Matt Ryan and myself supports Bauer's claim. We found that higher levels of economic aid depress economic freedom scores. Yet it is higher freedom that is necessary to attract investment and grow.

Aid and debt forgiveness will not promote the institutional environment of economic freedom and property rights that Africa needs to grow. Unfortunately, it is unlikely that Western nations can do much to get African nations to adopt pro-investment policies. President [George W.] Bush's Millennium Challenge Accounts [which increase development assistance to governments that show democratic and fiscal responsibility] pay lip service to this type of policy but the program has distributed little money and it is not clear that it would avoid the pitfalls of previous aid programs. Blair's call [in 2005] to double aid doesn't account for the importance of property rights at all.

G8 nations can still help, though. Instead of focusing on debt relief and aid, we should reform our domestic policies that harm the third world. The U.S. and E.U. [European Union] both protect our farm sectors from third world competition. Opening our borders to third world farm products would give an immediate boost to the standard of living in many poor countries. Blair and the G8 could do more to help the impoverished people of the world by freely trading with them instead of repeating failed policies of aid and debt forgiveness.

*"Evidence supports the notion that na-
tions more open to trade tend to be
richer than nations that are less open
to trade."*

Free Trade Would Help Africa

Marian L. Tupy

*Marian L. Tupy is the assistant director of the Project on Global
Economic Liberty at the Cato Institute, a libertarian public
policy organization. Tupy argues in the following viewpoint that
African economies would benefit from free trade, or trade liberalization. This economic philosophy suggests that trade goods
should be exchanged between countries with little government
intervention in the way of high tariffs or duties. Tupy contends
that African leaders want foreign governments to open their
economies to African goods but are unwilling to reduce the high
tariffs in their own nations. Tupy maintains that this protectionist policy is slowing trade between Africa and the rest of the
world and is also stymieing trade between African nations. Without opening their economies to imports, Tupy concludes, African
nations will not see significant growth and will remain mired in
poverty.*

Marian L. Tupy, "Trade Liberalization and Poverty Reduction in Sub-Saharan Africa,"
CATO Institute Policy Analysis, vol. 557, December 6, 2005, pp. 2, 8–11, 12–14, 18–19.

As you read, consider the following questions:

1. What was the gross domestic product (GDP) per capita "increase" in the sub-Saharan African region between 1975 and 2000, as Tupy reports?

2. In Tupy's view, how could Africa—which only comprises 0.6 percent of the global economy—harm the international economy and World Trade Organization (WTO) negotiations?

3. According to William Cline, as cited by Tupy, by what percentage would full trade liberalization reduce poverty in sub-Saharan Africa?

There is ample evidence that people have been trading with one another since the earliest times. As economists James Gwartney of Florida State University and Richard Stroup of Montana State University put it, the motivation for trade can be summed up in the phrase, "If you do something good for me, I will do something good for you." There are three important reasons why voluntary exchange is good not only for the contracting parties but for the world as a whole.

First, trade improves global efficiency in resource allocation. A glass of water may be of little value to someone living near the river, but it is priceless to a person crossing the Sahara. Trade is a way of delivering goods and services to those who value them most. Second, trade allows traders to gain from specializing in the production of those goods and services they do best. Economists call that the law of comparative advantage. When producers create goods that they are comparatively skilled at, such as Germans producing beer and the French producing wine, those goods increase in abundance and quality. Third, trade allows consumers to benefit from more efficient methods of production. For example, without large markets for goods and services, large production runs would not be economical. Large production runs, in turn, are instrumental to reducing the cost of a product. The reduction of the cost of production leads to cheaper goods and services, which increases the real standard of living.

Evidence supports the notion that nations more open to trade tend to be richer than nations that are less open to trade. As Columbia University economist Arvind Panagariya puts it: "On the poverty front, there is overwhelming evidence that trade openness is a more trustworthy friend of the poor than protectionism. Few countries have grown rapidly without a simultaneous rapid expansion of trade. In turn, rapid growth has almost always led to reduction in poverty." ...

Poor Economic Indicators

Nowhere is the need for poverty reduction greater than in sub-Saharan Africa [SSA]—a major part of the African continent that consists of 48 countries, spreads over 9.4 million square miles, and includes more than 700 million people. According to the UN Human Development Index [UNHDI], which measures human development or basic living standards on a scale from 0 to 1, with 0 being the lowest and 1 being the highest score, SSA's score was 0.468 in 2003. It was 0.655 in the developing world as a whole and 0.929 in the high-income OECD [Organization for Economic Cooperation and Development] countries. According to the UNHDI, SSA lags behind most of the world in practically all indicators of human well-being. The people of SSA suffer from shorter life spans; higher infant mortality; a higher incidence of HIV, malaria, and tuberculosis; a higher incidence of undernourishment; and lower school enrolment.

The region's growth record is poor. Between 1975 and 2000, GDP per capita in high-income OECD countries and the developing world increased at an average annual rate of 2.20 percent and 1.42 percent respectively. The comparable figure for SSA was negative 0.7 percent. In 2003, SSA's GDP per capita was US $513. Comparable figures for the developing world were US $1,289 and for the high-income OECD, US

$28,109. The percentage of people in SSA living on less than US $1 a day increased from 47.4 percent in 1990 to 49 percent in 1999.

High Tariffs

Regrettably, SSA continues to be one of the world's most protectionist regions. Under the Uruguay round [of World Trade Organization (WTO) talks from 1986 to 1994], developed countries agreed to slash their bound tariffs by almost 40 percent. In part because of a misconceived policy of special treatment for the least developed countries and their concomitant exception from some of the WTO rules, tariffs in SSA remained higher than in the rest of the world. . . .

In addition to tariffs, there is a plethora of nontariff barriers to trade that SSA countries employ. In 1998, Francis Ng and Alexander Yeats of the World Bank compiled a frequency ratio, which showed the percentage of tariff lines, or import items, subjected to nontariff protection. As with tariffs, low-income SSA scored higher (39 percent) than the developing world as a whole (23.5 percent). The nontariff barrier ratio for high-income non-OECD countries was 9.4 percent and for middle-income SSA, 13.7 percent.

The World Bank found that in 1997 SSA countries levied an average applied tariff of 34 percent on agricultural exports from other SSA countries. Industrial countries, by contrast, imposed an average applied tariff of 24 percent on SSA agricultural exports. Similarly, SSA countries maintained an average applied tariff of 21 percent on nonagricultural exports from other SSA countries. Industrial countries imposed an average applied tariff of 4 percent on SSA non-agricultural exports.

According to the WTO, only 10 percent of African (including sub-Saharan African) exports were intraregional (i.e., traded to other African countries). In contrast, 68 percent of exports from countries in Western Europe were exported to other Western European countries. Similarly, 40 percent of North American exports were to other countries in North America. It is notable that Western Europe and North America have regional trade agreements that allowed for a tariff-free and quota-free intraregional movement of goods. Though African trading blocs do exist, movement of goods is seldom free. Too often, the only tangible result of regional trade agreements in Africa is the creation of bloated and ineffectual bureaucracies. African protectionism is among the highest in the world, which partly explains why trade among African countries remains relatively low.

The Hypocrisy of African Leaders

Many African leaders have called for further trade liberalization. But, although they urge an end to protectionist policies in the developed world, African leaders refuse to open their own markets to foreign competition. For example, the African Union [AU] meeting in Libya in June 2005 called for "the abolition of [the developed world's] subsidies that stand as an obstacle to trade," but produced no concrete results on intra-African trade liberalization. Speaking at the AU meeting, Uganda's trade ambassador, Nathan Irumba, urged African leaders to "reject the straightjacket of radical tariff reductions, which would pose terrible risks for our domestic industries and jobs."

Similarly, South African president Thabo Mbeki called for an end to the U.S. and EU [European Union] farm subsidies. Referring to the September 2005 summit of leaders at the United Nations, Mbeki complained that the meeting had not achieved the necessary breakthrough on trade. "How serious is the developed world about this partnership to address this matter of poverty?" he asked. Yet, as a member of the Group of 21 developing nations (G-21), South Africa derailed the Doha round of [World Trade Organization] trade negotiations by walking out of the 2003 ministerial meeting in Cancun.

Eliminate Trade Barriers

Tariff and non-tariff barriers in developed countries pose a significant obstacle to developing country exports. While developed countries generally maintain relatively low average trade barriers, their highest trade barriers tend to apply to goods that developing countries export. The World Bank and Oxfam estimate that trade barriers erected by developed countries cost developing countries $100 billion a year. Non-tariff barriers also pose significant problems. For instance, agricultural subsidies encourage production and put downward pressure on agricultural prices. Michael Moore, former Director-General of the World Trade Organization, estimated that removing all tariff and non-tariff barriers "could result in gains for developing countries in the order of $182 billion in the services sector, $162 billion in manufactures and $32 billion in agriculture." The U.S. has partially addressed these trade distortions through AGOA [African Growth and Opportunity Act of 2000] and should commit to eliminating all remaining tariffs on goods from eligible nations and unilaterally phasing out agricultural subsidies.

Brett D. Shaefer and Daniella Markheim, Heritage Foundation WebMemo #1108, June 5, 2006. www.heritage.org.

As Alan Oxley, the former head of the General Agreement on Tariffs and Trade, explains, South Africa has moved away from trade liberalization in recent years. South Africa's negotiating position now more closely resembles ideas espoused by the British development and relief organization Oxfam, the Southern and Eastern African Trade Negotiations Institute, and a nonprofit organization called the Third World Network. Those organizations favor developed-world trade liberalization, while rejecting similar policies in the developing world.

In September 2005, for example, while the G-20 group (formerly G-21) was meeting in Pakistan, Oxfam issued a press release urging the group "to make sure [that] developing countries are not forced to cut their tariffs too quickly but retain sufficient flexibility to protect sensitive sectors."

Organizations such as Oxfam have been very influential, Oxley believes, in convincing the African bloc in the WTO in general and South Africa in particular of the need for domestic protectionism. An African return to protectionism would be bad news not only for African countries, but also for the future of the WTO. African countries aside from South Africa account for a mere 0.6 percent of global trade, but constitute the largest voting bloc in the WTO. If they succeed in derailing future trade negotiations, global trade could suffer.

Unfortunately, free trade continues to be misunderstood by many leaders in SSA and beyond. Perhaps the most important misunderstanding concerns the positive impact of foreign competition on stimulating domestic production. Imports are often seen as a threat, which is why SSA leaders emphasize exports and access to developed world markets as opposed to opening their own countries to foreign goods.

That view is mistaken. Imports increase specialization, and increased specialization leads to increased productivity. Reduction of the cost of production then leads to cheaper goods and services, which, in turn, increases the real standard of living. That is why people living in more open economies tend to be richer. As Mary O'Grady of the *Wall Street Journal* recently opined, "The beauty of free trade is that it increases competition. Preferential trade agreements may make a small segment of elite exporters better off. But it is importing—not exporting—that is the critical step in the process of wealth creation in the developing world. Access to low-priced inputs allows for productivity gains at home. Outside competition spurs innovation. Producers become more export competitive, as unilateral opening in both Chile and New Zealand have demonstrated." . . .

Estimated Benefits of Trade Liberalization

In a recent paper, Kym Anderson, Will Martin, and Dominique van der Mensbrugghe of the World Bank estimated the dollar value of SSA welfare gains resulting from full liberalization of global merchandise trade. Taking 2001 as the base year, the authors estimated that by 2015 annual welfare growth in SSA would be US $4.8 billion greater than it would have been had no trade liberalization taken place. However, it is notable that SSA welfare gains from global trade liberalization would be smaller than those of many other developing regions, including Latin America and the Caribbean, which would gain almost US $29 billion.

Moreover, World Bank research shows that SSA stands to gain from internal trade liberalization. Denis Medvedev of the World Bank's Development Prospects Group has estimated the welfare gains that SSA would receive from simple tariff liberalization among countries in SSA. He estimated that by 2015 annual welfare growth in SSA would be US $1.746 billion greater than it would have been had no intra-SSA trade liberalization taken place. That would amount to 36.4 percent of welfare gains that SSA stands to receive from full liberalization of global merchandise trade (US $4.8 billion). Intra-SSA trade would increase by 54 percent—an increase of US $12.6 billion.

According to the World Bank, "Even if Sub-Saharan Africa could turn falling per capita incomes into annual increases of 1.6 percent—an assumed baseline scenario—its rate of growth would be less than one-third the rate of growth that is expected in East Asia. The relatively poor performance of Sub-Saharan Africa makes the MDGs [millennium development goals] for that region especially challenging. For example, under the baseline scenario the percentage of people living on US $1 per day or less will be only 42.3 percent in 2015 instead of 24 percent as targeted by the MDGs."

[American economist] William Cline estimates that full trade liberalization would result in 20 percent poverty reduction across the world. According to Cline, out of approximately 2.75 billion people living on less than US $2 per day, 540 million could be brought out of poverty by 2015. However, he warns, "a greater share of poverty reduction . . . [would be] found in Asia and lesser shares in sub-Saharan Africa." Asia and SSA are the two poorest regions in the world, yet according to Cline's study, Asia would reduce its poor population by 23 percent, whereas SSA would reduce its poor by only 12 percent.

Trade liberalization in SSA, therefore, needs to be followed by domestic reforms, which are necessary to ensure that capital remains in SSA and is put to productive use there. As Arvind Panagariya observes: "While trade openness is empirically more or less necessary for rapid growth, it is not sufficient by itself. There are complementary conditions, such as macroeconomic stability, credibility of policy, and enforcement of contracts, without which the benefits of openness may fail to materialize."

"African countries have lost hundreds of billions of dollars in 20 years of liberalisation."

Free Trade Has Harmed Africa

Claire Melamed

Claire Melamed is head of the United Kingdom trade campaign at Action Aid, a charity that works with developing countries. She was a senior trade analyst for Christian Aid, another UK charity, when the following viewpoint—a briefing by that organization—was published. Melamed states that reports commissioned by Christian Aid found that the economies of impoverished sub-Saharan African nations have not improved after two decades of trade liberalization policies. She contends that when African nations open their economies to imports, their own producers and manufacturers suffer under the weight of cheap foreign goods. She asserts that the economic harm is felt most by the poorest Africans who depend on small farms and industries for their livelihood. With declining native production, African nations that embrace free trade end up relying more on foreign aid and thus never can build a strong enough infrastructure to begin climbing out of the poverty trap, Melamed concludes.

Claire Melamed, "The Economics of Failure: The Real Cost of 'Free' Trade for Poor Countries; a Christian Aid Briefing Paper," Christian Aid, June 2005. Reproduced by permission.

As you read, consider the following questions:

1. Why do free trade policies not typically raise exports of sub-Saharan nations, according to Melamed?

2. In the author's estimation, how much has trade liberalization cost sub-Saharan countries in U.S. dollars?

3. Why does free trade hurt poor farmers and workers the most, in Melamed's view?

As a major part of its remit to challenge systems that perpetuate poverty, Christian Aid has for many years given a voice to those harmed by trade liberalisation. We have highlighted the plight of farmers who are no longer able to sell their crops when cheap imports flood in and of people made jobless when factories close. These stories of the casualties of unfettered liberalisation need to be told, and we are proud of our role in giving a platform to those who otherwise would not have a voice in international debates.

However, supporters of liberalisation have always argued that these cases represent an unfortunate, but small, minority. They claim that the majority benefit from the new opportunities created by liberalisation. In this briefing, Christian Aid shows that this is not the case. Complementing our previous case studies, which show the devastation trade liberalisation wreaks on individuals, we demonstrate that whole countries would be much richer today if they had not been forced to open their markets.

Christian Aid commissioned an expert in econometrics to work out what might have happened had trade not been liberalised, using economic modelling. The work was reviewed by a panel of academics. The model looked at what trade liberalisation has meant for 32 countries, most in Africa but some in Asia and Latin America.[1]

The data came from the World Bank, International Monetary Fund, United Nations and academic studies. We established the year each country began to liberalise and the extent of its trade liberalisation. We used evidence on the impact of trade liberalisation on imports and exports, and the effect of this on national income, to estimate how much income was lost given the extent of liberalisation. The results suggested that:

- imports tend to rise faster than exports following trade liberalisation

- this results in quantifiable losses in income for some of the poorest countries in the world.

We are not arguing that countries which liberalise do not grow, or that some people in them do not become less poor but we are saying that without liberalisation, growth could have been higher and poverty reduction faster.

This report shows the true cost of the policies that have been forced on the developing world by donor countries and international institutions. The devastation import liberalisation has caused agricultural and industrial production in developing countries and the way it has severely limited their prospects of future development is well documented. This report puts a value on that loss.

What Poor People Have Paid For Trade Liberalisation

When trade is liberalised, imports climb steeply as new products flood in. Local producers are priced out of their markets by new, cheaper, better-marketed goods. Exports also tend to grow, but not by as much. Demand for the kind of things sub-Saharan African countries tend to export such as raw materials doesn't change much, so there isn't a lot of scope for increasing exports. This means that, overall, local producers are selling less than they were before trade was liberalised.

In the long run, it's production that keeps a country going and if trade liberalisation means reduced production, in the end it will mean lower incomes. Any gains to consumers in the short term will be wiped out in the long term as their incomes fall and unemployment rises.

This has been the story of sub-Saharan Africa over the past 20 years. Trade liberalisation has cost the 22 African countries in the modelling exercise more than US$170 billion in that time.[2] According to our model, this is the amount that the GDP [gross domestic product] of these countries would have increased had they not liberalised their trade in the 1980s and 1990s. If the model is applied to all of sub-Saharan Africa, the loss is US$272 billion.

While some countries in Africa have increased their GDP over the past 20 years, this increase is not as great as it could have been. There are more poor people in sub-Saharan Africa now than there were 20 years ago. Some of them would not be poor today, were it not for inappropriate trade liberalisation.

In the year 2000 alone, sub-Saharan Africa lost nearly US$45 dollars per person thanks to trade liberalisation. Most trade liberalisation in Africa has been part of the conditions attached to foreign aid, loans and debt relief. This looks like a bad deal: in 2000, aid per person in sub-Saharan Africa was less than half the loss from liberalisation only US$20. Africa is losing much more than it gains if aid comes with policy strings attached.

The staggering truth is that the US$272 billion liberalisation has cost sub-Saharan Africa would have wiped clean the debt of every country in the region (estimated at US$204 billion) and still left more than enough money to pay for every child to be vaccinated and go to school.

The negative effects of trade liberalisation are not confined to Africa. Low-income countries in Asia and Latin America have suffered similar consequences. The average loss to the countries in Christian Aid's study was about 11 per cent of total GDP over 20 years amounting to several billion dollars for each country. The total loss for the 32 countries in the study was US$896 billion.

How Trade Liberalisation Hurts
Poor Countries

Academic studies have shown that the main impact of liberalisation on trade flows is to increase the demand for imports at a faster rate than the demand for exports.[3] That is, following trade liberalisation, countries tend to buy more than they sell every year. As a result, their trade balance worsens and they have to live beyond their means, a situation which is not sustainable in the long term, without constant inflows of ever-increasing aid.

As imports increase, demand in the country for locally produced goods falls, because people are buying imported goods instead. The demand for exports doesn't increase enough to make up for the fall in local demand. For farmers, this will mean producing less, or selling at a lower price. For manufacturers, this might mean going out of business altogether.

As a result, developing countries could become increasingly indebted as they continue to spend more than they earn. However, poorer developing countries are highly unlikely to receive the finance (either loans, grants or investment flows) to fund this increased expenditure. Africa, for example, has been a net exporter of capital for much of the 1980s and 1990s.[4] Trade and finance liberalisation have been associated with increased capital flight from Africa. The problem has been compounded by reduced aid to Africa during the 1990s.

If more money doesn't come in from elsewhere, as aid, loans or foreign investment, the impact will be felt on GDP in the medium to long term. As demand for their products falls, local producers earn less, the total income of the country declines and imports eventually return to their pre-liberalisation levels all of which leads to a lower level of national income than would be the case without trade liberalisation.

Who Paid the Price?

If a country's GDP falls, it doesn't affect everyone equally. It is often the poor who suffer most. Recent evidence from the United Nations shows that countries which liberalised their trade most tended to suffer from increases in poverty. Countries that cut themselves off from trade altogether don't reduce poverty very successfully either; in fact, it was countries with moderate levels of protection that did best.

Anecdotal evidence supports this general trend. Christian Aid has produced numerous case studies over the years which show how poor people have been affected by trade liberalisation.[5]

- Tomato production used to provide rural households in Senegal with a good living. But after liberalisation, the prices farmers received for their tomatoes halved, and tomato production fell from 73,000 tonnes in 1990 to just 20,000 tonnes in 1997, leaving many farmers without a cash crop.

- In Kenya, both cotton farming and textile production have been hit. Cotton production, a key income earner for poor households, fell from 70,000 bales a year in the mid-1980s to less than 20,000 bales in the mid-1990s. Employment in textile factories fell from 120,000 people to 85,000 in just ten years.

- Rice imports in Ghana climbed to 314,626 tonnes per year following trade liberalisation. For local farmers, the results have been catastrophic. One of them told Christian Aid: 'One of the main problems we face is the marketing of our rice. We find it difficult to compete with imported rice on the market.'

As the examples above indicate, it is often poor farmers who suffer most when trade is liberalised. The fall in domestic demand which results from increased imports hits them particularly hard. Poor farmers have little access to capital or technology to increase their productivity or improve the quality of what they sell in response to more competition. They are also competing in an extremely unequal market, where imports from developed countries are often heavily subsidised.

Manufacturing industries have not grown up to employ people who are no longer able to make a living from farming. Instead, manufacturing has also been hard hit by trade liberalisation:

- In Zambia, employment in formal-sector manufacturing fell by 40 per cent in just five years following trade liberalisation.[6]

- In Ghana, employment in manufacturing fell from 78,700 in 1987 to 28,000 in 1993 following trade liberalisation.[7]

- In Malawi, textile production fell by more than half between 1990 and 1996. Many firms manufacturing consumer goods like soap and cooking oils went out of business, and the poultry industry collapsed in the face of cheap imports.[8]

A closer examination of import and export trends following liberalisation shows how this happened. In all the countries for which it had data, the UN Conference on Trade and Development (UNCTAD) found that, following trade liberalisation, imports of food increased as a proportion of all imports, while imports of machinery declined, again as a proportion of all imports.[9] The increase in cheap food imports priced farmers out of local markets. The relative decline in imports of machinery showed that manufacturers were also suffering; importing less machinery to run their factories, improve productivity and provide more jobs.

Trade liberalisation means a 'double whammy' for poor people, stifling the development of industry which would replace lost jobs in agriculture. Wherever they turn, poor people are hard hit by trade liberalisation.

Export trends bear this out. Though exports did increase in most cases following trade liberalisation, most countries simply exported more of the same; they did not start to export more manufactured goods, for example, or more higher-value agricultural exports. An UNCTAD study also found that many least-developed countries lost market share following trade liberalisation, as their exports failed to compete in international markets.[10]

It is clear that trade liberalisation is not driving the development of a more dynamic, diversified or pro-poor pattern of development. On the contrary, it is locking Africa into greater dependence on a few agricultural products whose prices have been declining for 50 years. Liberalisation is hitting manufacturing hard and it is the development of manufacturing that Africa needs if it is ever to trade its way out of poverty.

Conclusion

Trade liberalisation is not a good policy that has unfortunate consequences for a small minority of people. It is a policy imposed on developing countries by donors and international institutions that has systematically deprived some of the poorest people in the world of opportunities to develop their own economies and end poverty.

Poor people have been driven out of their domestic markets and found no international markets to compensate them. Development has stalled as industries have collapsed and imports of capital goods fallen, exacerbating the crisis in agriculture as fewer employment opportunities are available elsewhere.

African countries have lost hundreds of billions of dollars in 20 years of liberalisation. This means lost opportunities for education, for life-saving medicines and for investment in infrastructure and new industries. Instead, many African countries have seen increases in poverty. Trade liberalisation and those who have forced it on Africa must take its share of the blame.

What Can Be Done?

First, the drive to more liberalisation must stop. G8 [the top eight economies globally] countries must:

- Use their controlling stake in the World Bank and IMF [International Monetary Fund] to stop them forcing countries to liberalise trade as a condition of loans, grants and debt relief.

- Stop forcing countries to liberalise trade as a condition of bilateral aid and debt relief. As a first step, the UK should enact legislation to end the practice of demanding trade liberalisation as the price of UK aid.

- Support proposals in the WTO for special and differential treatment allowing developing countries not to implement agreements that are not in their interests. Second, developing countries must be allowed to roll back decades of liberalisation: they must be free to raise tariffs if necessary to meet development goals and technical advice offered to them by multilateral institutions or bilateral donors must include advice on the possible benefits of raising trade barriers as well as liberalising trade.

Country Examples

What trade liberalisation has cost Ghana. Ghana began to liberalise trade in 1986. In 2000, its gross domestic product (GDP) was just under US$5 billion. If Ghana had not liberalised, our model suggests that its GDP that year would have been nearly US$850 million higher. Adding the loss every year from 1986 to 2001 (the last year for which we have data) gives a total loss of nearly US$10 billion, or around ten per cent of Ghana's GDP over that period. In 2000, Ghana lost US$43 for every one of its 20 million people. In the same year, Ghana received aid worth just US$31 per person.

Over the 15 years since trade was liberalised, Ghana's population has lost the equivalent of US$510 per person—a huge sum, given that per capita GDP in 2000 was just US$330. It's as if everyone in Ghana stopped working for one and a half years.

What trade liberalisation has cost Malawi. Malawi began to liberalise trade in 1989. In 2000, its GDP was just over US$1.7 billion. If Malawi had not liberalised, our model suggests that its GDP in 2000 would have been more than US$1.9 billion US$200 million higher. Adding the loss every year from 1989 to 2001 (the last year for which we have data), gives a total loss of more than US$2 billion, or eight per cent of Malawi's GDP over that period.

In 2000, Malawi's population was 10.3 million and it lost more than US$20 per person thanks to trade liberalisation. In the same year, Malawi received aid worth US$43 per person.

Over the 15 years since trade was liberalised, Malawi's population has lost US$196 per person—a huge sum when you consider that per capita GDP in 2000 was US$165. It's as if everyone in Malawi stopped working for 14 months.

What trade liberalisation has cost Uganda. Uganda began to liberalise trade in 1991. In 2000, its GDP was nearly US$6 billion. If the country had not liberalised, our model suggests that its GDP in 2000 would have been over US$735 million higher than it was—more than what Uganda spent on health and education combined that year. Adding the loss every year from 1986 to 2001 (the last year for which we have data), gives a total loss of almost US$5 billion, or eight per cent of Uganda's GDP over that period.

In 2000, Uganda lost US$32 for every one of its 23.3 million people, thanks to trade liberalisation. In the same year, the country received aid worth just US$35 per person. Over the ten years since trade was liberalised, Uganda has lost US$204 per person compared with a per capita GDP in 2000 of US$253. It's as if everyone in Uganda stopped working for ten months.

What trade liberalisation has cost Mali. Mali began to liberalise its trade in 1991. In 2000, its GDP was US$2.4 billion. Our model suggests that, without trade liberalisation, the country's GDP would have been US$191 million higher in 2000 than it actually was—more than what Mali spent on healthcare during that year. Adding the loss over the ten years since Mali liberalised for which we have data, gives a total of US$1.4 billion.

In 2000, Mali's population was 10.8 million and it lost nearly US$18 dollars per person from trade liberalisation—more than half of the US$33 per person they received in aid. Since the early 1990s, Mali has lost nearly US$130 per person from trade liberalisation, or half a year's income. It is as if everyone in Mali stopped working for six months.

Notes

1. The countries in the study were: Bangladesh, Benin, Bhutan, Botswana, Burkina Faso, Cambodia, Cameroon, Cape Verde, Ethiopia, the Gambia, Guinea, Guinea-Bissau, Haiti, India, Indonesia, Kenya, Lao PDR, Madagascar, Malawi, Mali, Mauritania, Nepal, Nicaragua, Pakistan, Senegal, South Africa, Sudan, Tanzania, Togo, Uganda, Republic of Yemen and Zambia.
2. The information in the following section is taken from Egor Kraev, 'Estimating Demand Side Effects of Trade Liberalisation on GDP of Developing Coutnries', May 2005.
3. A U Santos-Paulino and A P Thirlwall, 'The effects of trade liberalisation on imports in selected developing countries', *The Economic Journal*, 114, February 2004.
4. J K Boyce and L Ndikumana (2001) 'Is Africa a net creditor? New estimates of capital flight from severely indebted Sub-Saharan African Countries', 1970–1996, University of Massachusetts.

5. See, for example, The Damage Done: Aid, Death and Dogma, Christian Aid 2005; Taking Liberties: Poor people, Free Trade and Trade Justice, Christian Aid 2004.
6. Neil McCulloch, Bob Baulch, Milasoa Cherel-Robson, 'Poverty, Inequality and Growth in Zambia during the 1990s', IDS Working Paper 114, Institute of Development Studies, University of Sussex, 2000.
7. Sanjaya Lall, Learning from the Asia Tigers, London: Macmillian, 1997.
8. Unctad, Least Developed Countries Report, 2004.
9. Ibid.
10. Ibid.

Periodical Bibliography

The following articles have been selected to supplement the diverse views presented in this chapter.

Robert Calderisi — "Africa: Better Off Without Us?" *New Statesman*, June 26, 2006.

Duncan Currie — "Aid Is Not Enough," *American Spectator*, November 2006.

Jason DeParle — "Preaching Free-Market Gospel to Skeptical Africa," *New York Times*, November 18, 2006.

Christina Cobourn Herman — "Jubilee," *Sojourners Magazine*, August 2007.

John Humphreys and Jane Conlon — "Fill Hearts, Minds and Bellies," *Times Higher Education Supplement*, October 5, 2007.

Tom Marchbanks — "The Phantom Menace," *New Internationalist*, August 2007.

New African — "How IMF, World Bank Failed Africa," January 2007.

Nicky Oppenheimer — "Why Africa Will Succeed," *New African*, July 2007.

Sam Rich — "Africa's Village of Dreams," *Wilson Quarterly*, Spring 2007.

Jeffrey D. Sachs — "A Global Coalition of Good," *Time*, September 17, 2007.

Rotimi Sankore — "'Not Enough Flies to Create the Right Effect,'" *New African*, July 2006.

Victoria Schlesinger — "The Continuation of Poverty," *Harper's Magazine*, May 2007.

Michela Wrong — "What Really Makes a Difference," *New Statesman*, June 4, 2007.

What Is the State of Democracy and Human Rights in Africa?

Chapter Preface

In July 2007 Human Rights Watch (HRW), an international watchdog organization, published a paper discussing the recruitment of children into the military and rebel forces fighting in Chad. Since 2005, Chad's government had been locked in war against insurgent groups, and according to HRW, "Children as young as eight serve as fighters, guards, cooks, and lookouts on the front lines of the conflict." Most of the children had been lured in by rebels promising money and security from the ethnic tensions that plague the nation, HRW contended. Even after peace agreements were signed between various rebel groups and the government in 2007, the recruitment of young boys continued. HRW asserted that one group, the United Front for Change (FUC), maintained its recruitment because as part of its peace deal, the rebels promised to fill the ranks of the government's army with replacement soldiers. In its report, HRW admitted that it "[did] not have evidence of ongoing recruitment of children on the part of the FUC, but girls and boys continue to serve in the FUC, and some children have fought alongside adult soldiers as combatants."

The use of children in warfare has gone on for decades in Africa. The most recent estimate (from 1999) places the number of child soldiers in Africa at 120,000. The United Nations notes that many militia groups and insurgent armies utilize children—primarily boys who range in age from seven to seventeen—"because children make for cheap and obedient fighters, and are easier—because of their youth and inexperience—to mold into effective and expendable combatants." Young girls are also lured or forced into warring armies to tend camps and serve as sex slaves to older soldiers. Critics charge that the pernicious practice continues because African governments are not made to crack down on the problem—

even as many of the national leaders sign international treaties against the use of child soldiers.

Organizations such as HRW argue that the recruitment of children into military or militia organizations is a violation of human rights. Amnesty International states that:

> The personal price paid by child soldiers is often high: brutalised and deeply traumatised by their [wartime] experiences, many continue to be haunted by the memories of the abuses they witnessed or were forced to commit. For girl soldiers, beyond the brutality and trauma of rape itself, sexual assault may result in serious physical injury and forced pregnancy, as well as infection with HIV or other sexually transmitted diseases.

To address the problem, the international community has passed legislation through the United Nations (UN) to outlaw the enlistment of child soldiers, and the International Criminal Court (ICC) has made the use of children under 15 years of age in combat a war crime. Many observers hope that these agreements—coupled with the local efforts of nongovernmental organizations that try to deprogram child combatants—will help reduce the number of children fighting in the wars in Chad and other parts of the continent.

In the following chapter, authors discuss other pressing human rights concerns in Africa. Some view the pressures of the UN and the ICC as necessary to guarantee human rights to Africa's people, who by and large have been subject to deprivations and ineffective—if not oppressive—governments since their colonization. Others suggest that human rights and the related democratization of Africa are faltering because international treaties and protocols rarely translate into practical, enforceable policies.

> *"Real, sustained efforts are being made across the continent to deepen democracy and reap the benefits of accountable governance."*

Democracy Is Proceeding in Africa

Jennifer Widner

Jennifer Widner is a professor of politics and international affairs at Princeton University. She is also the author of Building the Rule of Law. *She asserts in the following viewpoint that African nations are making progress toward democracy. Although Widner acknowledges that the continent is still plagued by corruption and electoral problems, she contends that several democratic elections have been held in various states and both governmental and public groups have initiated positive reforms to secure more civil rights.*

As you read, consider the following questions:

1. In Widner's view, what two things limit how far incumbent leaders can go in expanding their power over their people?

Jennifer Widner, "Africa's Democratization: A Work in Progress," *Current History*, vol. 104, May 2005, pp. 216–221. Copyright © 2005 by Current History, Inc. Reproduced by permission of Current History, Inc.

2. As Widner explains, what happened in Togo when the country's military sought to install Faure Gnassingbé in the seat of power left vacant by his father?

3. What does Widner claim that African nations will have to resist the temptation to do?

In February 2005, Nigerian commentator Mobolaji Sanusi referred to political developments in Africa as "demo-crazy." The target of his concern was the tendency of many of the continent's political leaders to set aside demands for serious competition and accountability and exploit elections by rigging ballots, changing constitutions to allow for longer terms, and ignoring other rules when convenient. [In 2005] several donor countries have expressed similar anxiety about the behavior of political elites in Nigeria, Kenya, Zimbabwe, Togo, Uganda, and many other countries, often taking to task reformers they had previously championed.

Anxiety About Democracy in Africa

This observation raises at least two important questions. The first is whether democratization has stalled in Africa, or whether the patterns to which Sanusi draws our attention simply reflect the last stands of the old-style authoritarian politicians, part and parcel of struggles to consolidate democratic reform. Certainly systematic regional backsliding is not all that evident, although movement toward more open systems has not accelerated either. Roughly 46 percent of sub-Saharan countries rank "four" or below on the Freedom House political liberties index (in which "one" indicates the highest standards of political rights and "seven" human rights standards on par with North Korea). Almost 19 percent of sub-Saharan countries rank "one" or "two" on this index. And during the past year four countries received better scores than they had the previous year, compared to three that received worse scores, including Zimbabwe. Since 2000, the overall ratings have changed relatively little. In 52 percent of countries, there was no change in the existing level of respect for political rights, while there was some improvement in 26 percent and some decline in 22 percent.

The second question is whether those governments that respect rights more now than in the past and hold regular elections perform any better than their predecessors. Much of the internal and external pressure for stronger observance of human rights and regular, competitive elections had its roots in the quest for accountable government. People in the street joined policy makers in reasoning that if citizens could vote against poorly performing politicians at the ballot box, political elites would have a stronger incentive to attend to the needs of ordinary citizens, choose policies that would generate economic growth, and reduce corruption. Greater respect for individual rights would also make it possible for information to circulate more freely, making corruption riskier, encouraging deeper discussion of policy issues, and drawing attention to problems, such as impending hunger, that left unaddressed would cause death or injury. Systematic information about state performance is hard to come by, but we do know that perceptions of corruption remain high in countries that have held elections and rank favorably on the Freedom House index of political and civil rights. Do these data suggest that our theories about the relationship between democracy and accountability are wrong, or does it just take time for the anticipated effects to materialize?

Progress Is Being Made

If the evidence suggests it is premature to answer these questions definitively, that in itself should give no cause for despair. Real, sustained efforts are being made across the continent to deepen democracy and reap the benefits of accountable governance. The success of these efforts has been mixed, but it is far too soon to write them off as failures. And, importantly, public participation in them is growing.

Pushing an authoritarian government to engage in political liberalization and hold multiparty elections is a difficult challenge. It requires not only an underlying sense of grievance or anger, but also people who are willing to assume the costs and risks of organizing others and relative weakness in the incumbents' ability to suppress or divert pressure for reform. Yet the tasks of consolidation, of building stable democracy, are if anything even greater, and although they may ease with time, they never go away. Most countries in sub-Saharan Africa not immersed in civil war have entered a difficult period: weak reform movements seek to maintain pressure on governments to adhere to promises, and responsive leaders are learning that to behave accountably they have to improve government capacity.

In any part of the world, incumbents and their entourages will try to hold on to power. How far they go toward that end is partly a function of popular and elite consensus on the rules and the bounds of appropriate behavior; it is also a function of the ability of civic groups and opposition parties to police and halt excesses. In sub-Saharan Africa, as in many places, we continue to observe problems with political norms, but overt violence at the polls as an intimidation tactic and tampering with ballot boxes are less common than they used to be. Africa, like other regions, suffers ever more sophisticated efforts to tip the electoral balance toward incumbents or toward the head of state's handpicked successor as consensus gels on norms against some of the most outrageous tactics.

Zimbabwe's Troubled Election

Zimbabwe's elections at the end of March 2005 anchored the negative end of the spectrum during the past year. Although the balloting was less overtly violent than at other times in the country's history, President Robert Mugabe sought to hold on to power by various means. He gained the right to appoint people of his choice to fill 30 of the 150 seats in the parliament. The government designed electoral boundaries to generate more safe seats for the ruling party. In the two years prior to the election, it arrested opposition leaders on several occasions and introduced a bill to ban human rights groups and other NGOs [nongovernmental organizations] that received any foreign funding. Youth groups attached to the ruling party engaged in political harassment, and there were reports of threats to deny food to those who voted against Mugabe. Journalists worked under increasingly tight restrictions after the 2002 Access to Information and Protection of Privacy Act gave the minister of information broad powers to confer or deny licenses for reporters and publications. When the elections were held, an estimated 10 percent of registered voters were turned away without being able to cast ballots.

Opposition groups inside and outside Zimbabwe tried to bring pressure on Mugabe to relent and to abide by the norms that govern free and fair elections. The country developed a spirited underground opposition, Zvankwana-Sokwanele ("Enough!"), which signaled its presence in different parts of the country with the spray-painted Bob Marley slogan, "Get up, stand up!" Demonstrations continued—although, during the lead-up to the vote, the police cracked down, breaking up most peaceful protests. The archbishop of Bulawayo, Pius Ncube, observed that the contest had been rigged before it started and urged Zimbabweans to follow the example of protesters in Ukraine. Mugabe responded to the archbishop by calling him a "halfwit." . . .

Other African Nations Stage Fairer Elections

Elections went off more smoothly in several other countries, suggesting that knowhow, norms, and accountability mechanisms may have improved in a broader regional context. In Ghana, John Kufuor won a second term as president in December 2004 with 53 percent of the vote and a turnout of 83 percent. Although the opposition objected to news of a coup plot—news it believed was designed to swing popular opinion in favor of the incumbent—the balloting was generally considered free and fair. Coup-prone Niger also conducted relatively free and fair elections in December 2004, returning President Mamadou Tanja to power for a second term. Ballots were helicoptered to insecure areas in the north, where security held for the duration of the election. Turnout was fairly low throughout the country, but the results were close in a hotly contested race. Coup master François Bozize ran for the presidency in the Central African Republic in an election that went off smoothly, although Bozize's candidacy met with disapproval in many quarters. In Cameroon's October 2004 elections, the picture was less happy than in Ghana and Niger, but fragmentation of the opposition was a greater cause for concern than outright manipulation of the vote that returned long-time president Paul Biya to office.

The Limits of Term Limits

Elsewhere political leaders have continued to employ another favored tactic for preserving their rule: trying to overturn constitutional limitations on terms of office. Earlier, leaders in Zambia, Malawi, Zimbabwe, Guinea, Togo, and Namibia had attempted to secure constitutional amendments to permit themselves to run for third terms. In Zambia and Malawi, public protest quashed these efforts, while in Zimbabwe, Guinea, Togo, and Namibia the bids to lift term limits succeeded.

[The year 2005] saw several more efforts of this type, including some from unexpected quarters. In April 2004, Namibia's president, Sam Nujoma, sought to amend the constitution yet again, this time to ensure that he could run for a fourth term. (He retired instead, ceding the presidency to Hifikepunye Pohamba, who was elected in November 2004.) In May 2004, the Burkina Faso legislature voted to amend the constitution to allow the head of state, Blaise Compaore, to remain in office for another term. Opposition parties attracted several thousand people to a protest demonstration in Ouaga-dougou, the capital, but some of the minor opposition parties allied with the government to pass the rule change. Gabon's parliament passed amendments allowing President Omar Bongo to run for office indefinitely. Bongo had already ruled for 36 years. In October 2004, Uganda's Yoweri Museveni, architect of the policies that helped move his country from civil war to donor darling, pushed to remove constitutional limits on the number of terms a president may serve. Although his intentions were not clear, this gesture would allow him to stand for election in 2006. Donor countries, international NGOs such as Transparency International, and civic groups within Uganda objected to the proposed constitutional alterations, and Museveni may still change his mind. . . .

Fewer Coup Attempts

Coups have become a less common means of securing power than in the past, thanks to concerted international efforts to cut off aid to countries whose leaders take office with the force of guns, and thanks to increasing domestic opposition. Togo tested this proposition on the death of President Gnassingbé Eyadéma on February 5, 2005. The country's military sought to install Faure Gnassingbé, Eyadéma's son, as president and forced a retroactive constitutional amendment through the legislature to make the move legal. Opposition parties immediately called for a two-day "stay at home" protest. A week later, demonstrators in Lome, Togo's capital, rejected the nonconstitutional transfer of power, and security forces killed three in the crowd. As Togolese protesters kept up the pressure domestically, people in neighboring countries took to the streets in support, and West African governments moved quickly to impose sanctions, despite a government promise to hold elections within 60 days. The sanctions set by the Economic Community of West African States included a recall of ambassadors, a travel ban on the Togolese leadership, and an arms embargo intended to help stem the importation of arms by the ruling party, which had already started to distribute weapons to its paramilitary supporters. The African Union followed suit. While the final outcome remains unclear, the strong regional and international response holds out the hope of curbing this attempt to evade the demands of democracy and accountability.

This quick inventory suggests that, although egregious efforts to circumscribe popular participation in politics are still occasionally evident and are likely to continue sporadically for some time to come, there are also growing signs of active domestic constituencies for accountable government. Demonstrations by civic groups are rarely if ever as large as those in Ukraine, Lebanon, and other countries outside Africa where citizens have tried to resist the usurpation of space for public dialogue, but they continue even in countries as traditionally inhospitable to such action as Togo. In some instances, such as the protests at the border of Zimbabwe, organizers have become increasingly creative in finding ways to communicate in the midst of oppression. With respect to democracy, the glass is half full.

Constitutional Conversations

At least as interesting as electoral conduct as an indicator of changing norms and patterns of behavior is the apparent belief among churchgoers, lawyers, politicians, students, and many ordinary Africans that diverse national communities must hold continuing conversations about the allocation of power and the fundamental rules of the game that will structure political life in the future. Since the mid-1970s, African countries have engaged in constitution-drafting exercises more than 90 times. Although some of these efforts were smokescreens for power grabs, many more were serious, participatory ventures. What is different about the tone now, compared

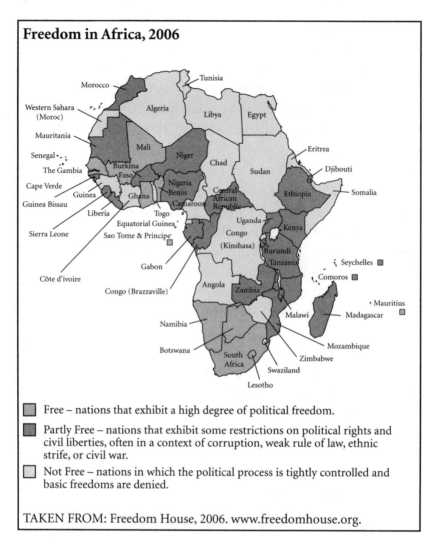

Freedom in Africa, 2006

■ Free – nations that exhibit a high degree of political freedom.

■ Partly Free – nations that exhibit some restrictions on political rights and civil liberties, often in a context of corruption, weak rule of law, ethnic strife, or civil war.

□ Not Free – nations in which the political process is tightly controlled and basic freedoms are denied.

TAKEN FROM: Freedom House, 2006. www.freedomhouse.org.

to earlier years, is that the process of reform is increasingly negotiated with civic groups and churches, instead of directed from the top, and nongovernmental organizations as well as opposition parties have persisted in monitoring deliberations and in lobbying for inclusion of important provisions.

[The year 2005] saw protests designed to move constitution-making processes forward in several countries. The most notable was popular action to try to shake up stalled deliberations in Kenya. In 1997, Kenyan opposition groups, religious leaders, and civic organizations launched a drive for constitutional change under the umbrella of the National Convention Executive Council. Pro-reform demonstrations in July 1997 were violently repressed and nine people died, while many others were injured. In 1998, the ruling party and opposition groups in the legislature hammered out a deal that set up a constitutional review commission and elaborated a five-part process. District forums and other bodies would nominate representatives to a national consultative conference. The government would then create a 26- or 27-member constitutional commission, with representatives of political parties, civic groups, religious communities, and women. The commission would sponsor hearings across the country and gather information. The 629-member national conference would weigh this information, and its recommendations would then go to a parliamentary committee for further review and presentation to the legislature, the body empowered by the existing constitution to adopt and ratify reforms.

Church-led protests kept the issue in the public eye through 1999, especially after the president, Daniel arap Moi, expressed his desire to keep the process within the national assembly—a procedure consistent with past practice but increasingly out of step with the more participatory processes employed across the globe. At one point civic and religious groups, which organized under the banner of Ufungamano, held their own conference and developed a draft. This coalition eventually won permission to nominate members to the constitutional commission. Its work informed deliberations at several stages. Other watchdog groups formed and continued to put pressure on the government to act through February and March of [2005].

The process slowed at several points, partly as a result of internal disputes and misaligned incentives, and partly because of meddling by the Moi government. Mwai Kibaki's

113

election as president in 2002 raised hopes of progress, but reform proposals remained mired in the parliament. Some of the disputes were substantive—for example, over the degree to which the president should share power with a prime minister. Others had roots in personal animosities and bids for influence. The president, then ill, had little inclination or ability to move the process forward. Rioting broke out in July 2004 as people grew increasingly impatient. Foreign diplomats and UN Secretary General Kofi Annan weighed in, reminding Kibaki to deliver on his campaign pledge to reform the constitution.

Popular action to push for constitutional dialogues has occurred in other countries as well. In Nigeria, President Olusegon Obasanjo's government has initiated a constitutional review process, arguing that the existing 1999 constitution was tainted by the influence of the military. Popular pressure helped put constitutional review on the agenda. The Electoral Reform Network, a coalition of 85 NGOs, has lobbied for renewed attention to the subject. The power to revise, adopt, and ratify a constitution lies with the legislature, but, like Kenya, Nigeria has broadened participation. The president created a National Political Reform Conference with 400 members, including delegates from each of the states, although preparation of draft language is in the hands of a committee of seven distinguished Nigerians. . . .

Dangers Ahead

Deep political change does not happen overnight. Sub-Saharan Africa is in an ambiguous transition period, with signs of hope as well as grounds for pessimism. Currently there are two main dangers.

The first ground for caution is the possibility that donor aid agencies, eager to show they have used their money to leverage change, will decide they have failed, prematurely, and pack their bags. That would be disastrous. Solid domestic and regional pressure groups are beginning to gain a toehold and initiate action in several countries. Usually they are still too weak to bring misbehaving officials to heel. Concerted regional and donor action is important for forcing leaders to respond to domestic demands. The case of Togo (though the story there is not yet over) shows what concerted internal and external pressure can achieve. The case of Zimbabwe shows what happens when regional powers avert their eyes.

Accountable government is not something achieved by the "simple" creation of a competitive electoral process. It is the joint effect of several conditions, not all of which are yet present. Voters cannot send clear signals by voting out the bad guys unless they care about politics, know who is responsible for policies or practices they dislike, and can sort out performance from the many other attributes of a candidate they may find attractive or unattractive. Eliminating coercion in the polling process and giving candidates a level playing field are both important, but they are not all that matters. For most ordinary people in most countries, it is hard to acquire all the information necessary to cast a ballot thoughtfully. Instead, people tend to take cues from members of the "interested public" whom they respect—public intellectuals they trust or like, or organizations that represent people like them, kin groups for example. These people pay closer attention to politics and policy and their positions offer cues to those with less time, motivation, or capacity to make judgments. A challenge for many African countries is to create an environment in which nonsectarian groups that perform these functions can acquire information, communicate freely, and establish ties with rural majorities. Young political elites in some countries already play these roles, but in other places this group is small and constrained. . . .

Finally, accountability is partly a function of the government's ability to respond. Since the 1970s, donors have often neglected capacity building, believing that money spent on training public officials, building facilities, or working closely with ministries is money in the hands of the corrupt or the abusive. Although the reluctance to work directly with governments is understandable, it is increasingly inappropriate in countries where civic groups can criticize openly and where the ability to monitor the use of resources has improved. A government cannot respond effectively if it lacks personnel able to do so or if it cannot manage its fuel supply well enough to send judges or other officials throughout the country.

Resisting Temptation

Strengthening the causal relationship between democracy and accountability will depend on external events too—and here is where the second danger arises. The next decade is likely to see competition between China and the West to buy Africa's oil. Already we have seen signs in Sudan that competition for oil has made some countries, including China, unwilling to press a government to behave responsibly toward its citizens. Willingness to keep quiet about abuses while paying cash on the barrelhead gives some purchasers an advantage over others. Ultimately this willingness to trade without regard for who gets the money or how it is used may undermine international and regional coalitions for good government and help generate high levels of conflict on the African continent. It would be unfortunate if a short-term quest for energy returned the world to the days in which Africa was nothing more than a source of primary commodities. Africans and their friends abroad should resist the temptation to trade recent tentative advances in pursuit of better governance for money and a renewal of the exploitative relationships of the past.

"*Perhaps many African societies are not ready to become democracies.*"

Democracy Is Faltering in Africa

Sebastien Arnold

In the following viewpoint, Sebastien Arnold states that democracy has not succeeded in many African countries. He blames this on the poor fit between Westernized democracy and African cultural values. He also claims that democracy has been stymied in Africa by powerful autocratic regimes, lack of public education on the electoral process, and the fledgling nature of pro-democracy groups. Sebastien Arnold is an exchange student from Switzerland who is now attending Harvard University.

As you read, consider the following questions:

1. When and where did the "great wave" of democracy begin in Africa, according to Arnold?

2. Why does Arnold believe that the "illnesses of democracy" in Africa are not a temporary phase between one system of government and another?

3. In the author's view, why do African people have little interest in governance?

Sebastien Arnold, "Democracy: A Universal Human Rights Pill?" *Earth Focus*, Summer 2006. Reproduced by permission.

When our grandparents' generation founded the United Nations and printed what became the Universal Declaration of Human Rights, they understood that the greatest challenge of the New World was perhaps not the material reconstruction of wartime damages, but the remodeling of the collective minds that had allowed history's greatest butchery to take place. The pre-emptive measures of Versailles [where the peace agreement was signed to end World War I] had not only failed to be effective but had nurtured a new crisis; a bold new course had to be taken to ensure that such a mistake would never be made again. The battle against Hitler had left a world which, albeit materially ruined, presented a great opportunity for change. What if the best way to ensure sustainable peace was not to punish yesterday's wrongdoers and alienate them, but to create a fairer society with equal opportunities for prosperity based on the values of self-determination and equality? Such a plan was an extraordinary use of victor's power! And so these ideals, formulated by [British prime minister Winston] Churchill and [U.S. president Franklin] Roosevelt as early as 1941 in the Atlantic Charter, spurred the western powers, with the world at their feet, to create this brave new world with Africa as a test bed. Sixty years later, have the seeds of democracy burgeoned in Africa? Has it managed to uphold human rights; is it sustainable?

The Fleeting Promise of Freedom

Certainly, the efforts have been relentless. A great wave started by the independence of Ghana in 1957 ended with the gaining of Eritrean autonomy from Ethiopian rule in 1993 as the last vestiges of colonialism were destroyed. European states granted self-determination to their colonies en masse. Much has changed since the Beatles made the world sing along to Yesterday—in the 1960's. Today, after decades of blood, toil, tears and sweat, most of these countries have democratically-elected governments and are progressing towards free market economies, in a move to imitate their successful northern counterparts. Forget about Yesterday; today is a Brand New Day.

However, if things should seem positive superficially, in many cases, the situation is less clear-cut. Perhaps the words of John Lennon and his band were unwittingly prophetic; the lyrics "yesterday all my troubles seemed so far away" sadly sound very true to many of these peoples confronted by their new reality. The truth is often in contrast to the façade we wish to see. In many places, democracy brought dreams of Utopia, but never realised them. No African country has seen an evenly spread improvement in living standards; in fact, in real terms, some of them were richer 20 years ago than they are now. Rich, age-old cultures have been pillaged in an attempt to unite under one flag in the name of freedom and independence a people that is in fact an arbitrary union of various peoples. [Côte d'Ivoire president Felix] Houphouët-Boigny's concept of 'Ivoirite' has unified a nation but excluded thousands. It seems that few, if any, of Africa's democracies have worked for the benefit of all.

The temptation is great to qualify these illnesses of democracy as a temporary adaptation phase between one system of governance and another: but such a discourse would only mask the realities. Democracy has been in place there for decades already and in some cases acts as a covert threat to human rights, because the governments have functioned ineptly. Two-tiered systems have often been created between small westernised elites who have adhered to the idea and benefited from it, and the rest who have been kept aside because they did not understand it. Moreover, the democratic governments often failed to deal with many pressing issues. In South Africa for instance, a decade after the end of apartheid, the land ownership situation is virtually unchanged and the disparity between whites and blacks remains alarming. If democracy cannot answer the people's plight, will the South Africans solve their issues like the Zimbabweans [i.e., with violence]?

Certainly, these are temporary illnesses, but with long-lasting consequences. If democracy consistently fails to realise these dreams, even for whatever valid reasons, the population's faith in the system will weaken and the foundations of human rights will be undermined. Should we be reminded that the USSR, Third Reich and People's Republic of China, three of the greatest foes of the values of human rights, were the unwanted pregnancies of failed democratic governments?

Forcing Western Democracy to Fit Africa

So is democracy a killer of human rights? Certainly not: the concept of democracy is not the problem. In the West, no other system has protected our human rights as well as democracy; it is indeed the least bad form of government. But that is the case in our culture. In many ways and for many reasons, exporting democracy abroad in haste was nothing other than a naïve idea. A Western ideal has been imposed with little consideration for the culture, history, and sociological make-up of the continent. Upon independence, the parliament of Ghana has been modeled on Westminster. But is Ghana anything like the United Kingdom? Certainly not! Sociologically, the United Kingdom is a monochrome compared to the ethnically complex Ghana. It is therefore not surprising if the Ghanaian democracy, like many others, has undergone much turbulence since its creation.

The key fact is simple: the functioning of a democracy relies wholly on several foundations that these newly democratic countries cannot provide. For one, the very foundation of democracy is that the will of the majority prevails. Such an ideal is straightforward and valid in an ethnically homogenous country like the United States, where nearly 80% of the population is of European descent. You can freely choose between Republicans and Democrats, but ultimately, you're still voting for one of your group. What about Africa, land of cultural diversity? A country like South Africa speaks 11 tongues; others,

Elections Staged for Show

Democratization in Africa is losing its connection with the real lives of African people, as the exercise of power is reconfigured to satisfy minimal international requirements of periodic elections. Electoralism has come to consume democratic efforts to the detriment of broader and more systematic transformations. "Africa is not being served," one observer has contended, "by the unseemly scramble for state power and resources that passes for elections in much of the continent." Periodically, electoral dances are staged by autocrats like Blaise Campaoré of Burkina Faso, Gnassingbé Eyadema of Togo, Paul Biya of Cameroon, Meles Zenawi of Ethiopia, and even Charles Taylor of Liberia—all in the absence of very basic conditions for fairness and political freedom. In the particularly wretched case of Togo, Gnassingbé Eyadema [who died in 2005] extended his 36 years in power by being consecrated president after "elections" on 1 June 2003, having swept aside the democratic movement of the early 1990s, bulldozed through two presidential elections, eliminated the constitutional two-term limitation, and erected procedural barriers for his most potent adversary, Gilchrist Olympio.

Richard Joseph, Journal of Democracy, *July 2003.*

like those of East Africa, are so diverse that they need to teach a trade language at school to enable peoples to talk to one another. In most cases, the biggest ethnic group has less than half of the total population. As each ethnic group votes for a party that represents it, in many cases a minority can govern the country all the time. For example, in Namibia, a party drawing its strength mostly from the Ovambo tribe has been in power ever since independence; other parties are widely deemed to have virtually no chance of gaining power. Many countries are still governed by a minority, just as they were before: the danger is that the governments are now authoritative and legitimate, with the full powers accorded to democratic governments. If even the will of the majority, the very basis of democracy, is not fulfilled, how can democracy work?

Prevalence of Ruling Parties

Democracy secondly depends on the notion of sharing power and regular changes in leadership. Any democracy would be nothing if it was not for the idea of competition: the best party gets the vote. If a leader fails to perform, let him be changed! However, this consumerist tendency is counternature to many cultures with a different approach to their leaders. For a variety of reasons, many Africans have an unswerving faith in their leader and need him to be strong. Sociologists have, for example, long suggested a link between family structures and leadership. African nations have but a recent history of independence; they still have their own George Washingtons, fathers of their nation to whom they are indebted. Democratically elected leaders span decades in Africa, because the citizens vote for continuity. These leaders then become half-Gods, Kwame Nkrumah, Ghana's first Prime Minister and despot, remains a great symbol of freedom, and Julius Mwalimu Nyerere, the longest serving head of a Commonwealth state, is respected enormously by all Tanzanians despite his catastrophic ujamaa farming programme. His party is still in power today, despite the empowerment of opposition parties. Objectively, Zimbabwe would hugely benefit from a change in leadership: however, although [president Robert] Mugabe probably falsifies election results, it would be naïve to claim that his support is not widespread. He will forever be remembered as the one who lead Zim' to independence. In Africa, the leader is the Leader. He is sacred, cannot be changed.

Lack of Interest in Politics

There are many potholes on the way to democracy in Africa. Education is an obvious stumbling block. The first obstacle is naturally a political immaturity; democratic systems of governance are still a recent import to Africa, and the populations are not accustomed [to] the mechanisms. Many of the non-Western educated citizens cannot understand the system or their power as individuals. This is hardly an African symptom; a quick look at how the French dealt with their once-in-a-decade referendum opportunity shows that political immaturity is widespread. This will take time to overcome. The second one is the population's lack of interest in politics. Many African peoples pay little interest to governance, because they cannot benefit from it. The government's economic growth policies will not make the Maasai farmer have more cattle; yet that is how his economic system functions. Consequently, interest groups cannot form, although they are vital to a democracy. The Indian democracy works well because there is a civil society and industrial lobbies behind it. This can only happen once the population has wealth to protect; but many tribes do not consider a paper bill to be wealth.

Democracy Is Not Suited to All

So perhaps many African societies are not ready to become democracies. Perhaps they had always considered that the best way to ensure their own prosperity and justice was the system that had been in place for centuries before the Europeans meddled with it: a mosaic of different ethnic groups, with different interests and different leaders, looking after themselves on their own. If democracy currently fails to work in Africa, it is not just because they are not educated, but for a variety of reasons embedded in the people's culture. One size does not fit all. The irony is that, today, Africa is not the only place in which democracy is not functioning well. Much of the population of the former Warsaw Pact countries, especially those in the primary and secondary industries, took a serious beating after the fall of communism, and nostalgia is alive. Our view of the East is masked by the up-and-coming generation of yuppies that has exploited the change to make considerable fortunes. More recently, efforts to install democracies in Afghanistan and Iraq, places historically governed by warlords and tribal councils, have so far proven completely disastrous. The governments are the least credible, least influential, and least stable the countries have seen in living memory. Perhaps in those cases it was unwise to impose democracy overnight?

It seems that after the Second World War the Western powers were swept by a wave of idealism, and came to believe that what had worked well for them would work for the whole of humanity. Over the past 200 years, millions of Americans, Europeans, Australians and New Zealanders have fought and died in the name of democracy. We are one with the ideal and would sacrifice anything to defend it and uphold its values. Unsurprisingly, the societies that have received democracy rather than earned it cannot relate to it in the same way and cannot find the momentum needed to make it work. The idea that democracy is the only way to prosperity seems very one-dimensional; rather, it would appear that any system can do, as long as the people believe in it: it is up to the societies to find that system on their own.

So should we continue to impose democracies to uphold the values of human rights? We could do worse without democracies but maybe other nations might do better without.

> *"If meaningful democracy is to become a force for real change in our continent, then we must empower our people to make it their own."*

Africa Needs Its Own Brand of Democracy

Jerry Rawlings

In the following viewpoint, Jerry Rawlings, the former president of Ghana, argues that African democracies must be devised and nurtured by Africans. He maintains that Western notions of democracy should not define African democratic order. Instead, he contends that Africans should build upon the institutions that have served Africans well while adhering to the principles of community, broad consensus, and social cohesion that are the strengths of African culture. In this way, Rawlings hopes that Africans will achieve participatory democracy in which the people are empowered to take on civic leadership roles and share in the burdens of building a just society. Jerry Rawlings was installed in power by a military coup in 1979. He quickly returned power to a civilian government within three months. He again came to power in 1981 after deposing the civilian government and establishing a twenty-year rule. During part of that rule (1993–2001), he was the legally elected president of Ghana.

Jerry Rawlings, "Facing the Challenges of Democratic Reform in Africa," *eAfrica*, September 2005. Reproduced by permission of the SA Institute of International Affairs.

As you read, consider the following questions:

1. What does Rawlings say he means when he advocates "reform"?

2. Why does Rawlings say that he has been sometimes accused of being against democracy?

3. What are the four basic elements of democracy that Rawlings believes are desirable requirements for every civilized society?

Africa's political history since independence has largely been characterised by a scarcity of verifiable documentation and a dearth of information on the activities of the key players in the struggle for liberation and democratic evolution.

Leaders such as Patrice Lumumba an [anti-colonialist and first elected prime minister of the Republic of the Congo] never had the opportunity to contribute to our knowledge of Africa's political development because their lives were cut out prematurely by the anti-liberation forces of their time. The few who committed their thoughts to writing, such as President Kwame Nkrumah [of Ghana] did so in exile, and could hardly avoid some sense of bitterness and self-justification. It is only in recent years that some African leaders have been able to collect their thoughts after leaving office, without fear of reprisal.

The chequered political history of many of our countries has led to the loss of a great deal of archival material, which could have influenced subsequent political developments in our countries. This, in turn, has made it easy for successor-regimes to distort the immediate past to their advantage.

Now that a growing number of African countries are moving towards some sense of continuity in governance, with relatively peaceful and democratic transfer of power, it is imperative that this process be strengthened by the building of collective sources of material.

It is only when our electorates are armed with true, factual and objective information about our political past that they can make informed decisions and see through attempts at misinformation.

The history of our continent, for the better part of the 20th century, was engrossed by the struggle to move beyond colonialism and the last vestiges of racist control and arrogance.

In spite of the traumatic experiences of post-colonial Africa, political independence and relative self-determination remain the struggle's most important achievements of Africa in the same period.

Redefining the Relationship with the West

African countries, which had hitherto been clients of a bipolar world, have had to face a new challenge: that of adopting a new set of responses to impulses coming from the West.

Autocracies have had to be quickly dismantled; frozen centralised economies are opening up, while relationships with multilateral institutions are similarly being realigned and redefined. In short, Africa has had to, as it were, reinvent itself and learn new ways of doing business with a changing world. That challenge lingers and is one of the defining characteristics of the present.

African countries will make progress, depending on the degree to which their national leadership can come to terms with and re-direct their national affairs in line with these imperatives.

It is also gratifying that in so short a time, the indications of positive change in Africa have been encouraging. New democracies are taking hold in different parts of the continent. Concurrently, existing 'democratic' governments that had been virtually one-party states have opened up the political space and have embraced reforms, albeit often reluctantly.

This brings us to another defining challenge, that of moving beyond mere forms and institutions of democracy as defined by Washington and Westminster to make it meaningful to the ordinary people of Africa. Meaningful participatory democracy must involve our people in day-to-day decision-making, as it did in most African cultures in pre-colonial times and still does to some extent in our traditional areas. Voting once every few years is just a part of what true democracy should be.

If we settle for meeting the basic criteria of democracy as prescribed by the West, we will find ourselves dealing with a façade behind which very undemocratic power is wielded to the benefit of a political elite. . . .

Building on What Exists

As I see it, the basis of the African re-awakening must be a rigorous reform of our economies and governments. Such reform, in order to be meaningful, must be informed by a radical change in our perceptions. We must critically question all received assumptions, overturn moribund institutions and jettison counter productive beliefs, be they alien or indigenous.

This brings us to a fundamental question: Between economic reform and political democracy, which should come first? That is one question that begs for an answer as African countries are made to fall over each other in the scramble to impress creditors by embracing westernised formal democracy.

What do we mean by 'reform'? I shall take it to mean amending and improving existing institutions and policies to better perform their functions in furtherance of the sustainable well-being of the people, and where necessary, thinking 'outside the box' of external prescriptions.

Too often on our continent, 'reform' means demolishing useful indigenous culture, jettisoning long-term objectives, removing competent administrators, technocrats, board members for no other reason than that they are perceived as connected to a previous regime.

This is the destructive face of reform, which has abruptly interrupted long-term programmes designed to benefit future generations.

To me, 'reform' should mean building upon what exists, but with an open mind to reshaping it where it is necessary to refocus and to realign.

Reform means change. Change is simply replacing one set of conditions by another. It may be positive or negative. It may be motivated by nothing more than boredom with the status quo or a genuine response to an intolerable situation.

Change in itself is neither good nor bad, but any change carries a cost. Since change disrupts the status quo, it is necessary to weigh the cost of reorganisation after disruption, and the consequences of interrupted programmes and policies. Obviously, it is only when change is for the better that these costs can be justified.

Democratic change could also mean change brought about by democratic means. Such change is not necessarily good even if the process by which it is brought about is acceptable. For example, elections may be held and adjudged free and fair by the most objective of observers and yet bring about a change which is to the detriment of the generality of the people.

In countries such as ours, where many people still exist on the edge of desperate poverty, and where there is a large deficit in education, it is easy to promise the electorate the moon if only they will democratically endorse change. It is also easy to temporarily corrupt the electoral process.

Those countries which have appointed themselves our 'tutors' in democracy (whilst undemocratically threatening us with withdrawal of aid if we do not swallow their forms of democracy whole) will say that such a 'democratic mistake' does not matter because at the end of the term of office of

Keeping Colonialism Alive

It is not possible to say definitively why post independence leaders failed to find and develop new models from their societies' political heritage. However it is a fact that many of postcolonial African leaders had been uprooted from and become ignorant of their cultural roots and philosophy. Many were exposed from a young age to colonial education systems and political propaganda that held that Africa had no history, no social systems and no political heritage to build on. Further, these future leaders were impressed by a western political system that appeared, on the surface at least, to offer an effective path to power and wealth and that this system was universal, timeless and applicable everywhere.

On this basis, the aim of independence, it appears, was not to do away with the system, but to replace the white governors with black presidents. This was the main reason for keeping the system, the colonial language and the colonial borders intact. In these artificial borders they could build perverted images of their colonial system. There was no attempt to adapt the political organization to the African reality and needs. The result has been chronic political instability, coups and counter-coups, pervasive corruption and underdevelopment, which has led in some cases to brutal internal conflicts and sometimes to genocide.

Garba Diallo, Holler Africa! August 5, 2007.
www.hollerafrica.com.

that government, it can be democratically voted out. Meanwhile, the crimes and human rights abuses, killings and tortures are shamefully treated with the case of the three monkeys—see no evil, hear no evil, speak no evil!

A Need for Participatory Government

What those prosperous countries fail to acknowledge is that for people living at the edge of existence as we do, four years of misery is a long time. When people become desperate, social norms and order may be subjected to immense stress, leading to the destruction of the fabric of society—especially when the judiciary becomes subservient to the executive.

Change brought about by democratic processes, or at least the forms of democratic processes which bear the seal of approval of the present world order, can therefore be either good or bad, depending to a large extent on how well informed the electorate is and the ability of the average voter to make reasoned choices.

I would, in the African context, prefer to define democratic reform as change which enhances democracy in the sense that it provides broader opportunities for more citizens to be involved in the process of governance.

What I would call participatory democracy goes beyond the periodic right to vote. It goes beyond lining the electorate up behind political parties in order to determine winners and losers. It means getting ordinary men and women involved in the day-to-day decision-making of grassroots governance in their communities to the extent that they feel that their actions can influence events.

I have known from personal experience, both when I was at the bottom and when I became a Head of State, that if we could decentralise some of the burdens and the responsibilities carried by the central government and share these responsibilities with the people by empowering them with some of the economic and political authority that a growing percentage of our citizens would become real participants in governance, understanding the hard realities of development and progress and sharing in successes and difficulties. Both the governed and governors, therefore, end up taking responsibility for the right and wrong policies.

This means encouraging an active sense of ownership and pride rather than a passive feeling of helpless acceptance of whatever is decided by the government. It means nurturing a spirit of positive defiance, a readiness to confront that which is clearly wrong and which undermines the building of a just society.

Confronting What Is Wrong

I have sometimes been accused of being against democracy because I have said that the people's involvement in governance must go beyond the ballot-box, and because I have expressed concern about the tendency of multi-party politics, especially on our continent, to become antagonistic and divisive, to foster a cynical kind of expediency which owes more to prospects of the next election than it does to the long-term interest of the people, and makes politics too dependent upon which group has more money.

When I speak about positive defiance, it may seem that I am stoking flames of civil disobedience. No. I mean a readiness to confront that which is clearly wrong and which undermines the building of a just society. If our people lose the courage to confront what is wrong then we become collaborators.

Let me reiterate quite clearly that I am a passionate believer in democracy. This is why I am more concerned about the essence of democracy than about the outward forms of democracy. We must infuse those forms with the spirit of the people. They must own democracy; they must feel a part of it. That is the only way democracy can thrive on our soil.

Let me also say that I believe that my concerns about partisan politics are valid. This does not mean, however, that I am saying that the multi-party system must be abandoned. It means that all of us, the electorate and the political parties—whether in power or in opposition—must endeavour with all sincerity and strength of will to avoid the latent negative tendencies which can so easily distort multi-party democracy, and turn it into a mere cloak of political respectability to hide the misuse of money, power and influence to benefit a political group to the detriment of the long-term interests of society as a whole and of the disadvantaged in particular.

Birth Pains of Independence

In Africa, independence from the colonialists was gained without the necessary empowerment of the majority yet they were required to adopt the democratic norms of the metropolitan countries a day after the colonialist flag was lowered. The masses of Africa were thus thrown into political independence and Western democracy at the same time. It was this situation that produced the political convulsions of the immediate post-colonial era.

Today again, the logic of world history has led to the projection of Western-style multi-party democracy as a universal model. Every country is now to be measured in terms of whether their political system approximates the classical Western model. More dangerously, adoption of this brand of democracy has suddenly become the criterion for either debt forgiveness or new grants or loans. Very little effort is being made by the champions of this universal democracy to accelerate the economic development of those parts of the world that have obvious difficulty in embracing this foreign type of democracy. Also, very little effort is being made to understand the cultural and historical peculiarities of these diverse societies.

To my mind, the very essentials of democracy are in themselves desirable requirements for every civilised society. These include respect for the basic freedoms and responsibilities, the rule of law, due process, orderly succession. I, however, refuse to accept the claim that there is only one model of democracy that ought to command universal application, as, indeed, no one model has as yet been known to be above blemish. What is called for is a creative adaptation of the basic principles of democracy to the local peculiarities of different societies. The cultural and historical diversity of Africa dictates this imperative. Perhaps what we need to be speaking about is 'Appropriate Democracy'.

In South Africa, for instance, centuries of white rule dictated a different constitution from what we adopted in Ghana, where racial discrimination has not been as destructive an issue in our history, outside the slave trade.

It is possible to see how some conflicts and tension in some parts of Africa are traceable to the rigid application of divergent interpretations of democracy to heterogeneous societies.

Most African economies are still caught in a web of contradictions, with a constant crisis of expectations between what the West expects as the natural outcome of an election in Africa and what actually happens. This is one reason why foreign observers of elections in Africa's new democracies always come out perplexed.

A political system predicated on poverty cannot yield fair results or engender fair play, especially when a sitting government makes it its preoccupation to subordinate the spirit and corrupt the moral fibre of a people.

Africans Must Follow Their Own Path

In today's troubled world, the concerns of Africa have often been marginalised. But we Africans, who daily experience those concerns, have no excuse to relent in the struggle to empower our peoples to harness the rich human, economic and natural resources of our continent to provide social justice and self-development in peace and dignity. Thankfully, a growing concern for Africa in some international circles has led to a movement towards some relief of the inequities which have held us back.

But the models of democracy which are held up before us for admiration and emulation, and by whose yardstick we are judged according to how closely we copy them, have themselves become rather threadbare.

It is no secret that these models are themselves riddled with unethical and self-serving practices and the influence of money, and that the electorates of these 'model democracies' have become cynical and apathetic about their political systems, if not outright antagonistic.

Let us therefore fashion our own path, one which will foster true, meaningful and participatory democracy in the nations of Africa. And let us have the courage to speak out in the world about global wrongs instead of seeking to please major powers for the sake of a few aid dollars.

But to do this, we and nobody else, must answer the question of why, for example, we cannot address the problems of bureaucratic inefficiency and apathy in our own countries, of pervasive corruption, of sudden eruptions of ethnic or religious violence, of the erosion of moral values, of mindless lawlessness. We debate and discuss, exhort and preach. But we do not get to the roots of the problems and so we do not act appropriately.

Democracy Rooted in African Culture

If meaningful democracy is to become a force for real change in our continent, then we must empower our people to make it their own. To impose 'democracy' from above is a contradiction of terms. It must be a process whereby ordinary men and women voluntarily take on the responsibility to speak and act for the good of the broader community. Where this is ignored or suppressed, resentments will build and will sooner or later lead to another cycle of disruption. Let us once again learn from history, and from the world around us today.

I believe that the real roots of democracy in Africa derive from the best aspects of our traditional systems of governance. Whilst we reject the outdated and negative aspects, such as superstition, attitudes and prejudices towards women, family planning, we need to build upon the positive. The traditional spirit of community, of building broad consensus, of social cohesion, of the right of the humblest citizen to voice his or her concerns before the council of elders—all these and more can help us fashion a participatory democracy which is rooted in our own cultures, rather than modelled on the historical experiences of other continents. I am not advocating a divergence from the basic principles of internationally accepted democracy, but rather a marriage of ideas which will produce systems which our people perceive as their own.

| *"The realization of economic, social and cultural rights remained illusory in virtually all countries in Africa."*

Africa Suffers from Human Rights Abuses

Amnesty International

In the following viewpoint, Amnesty International—a global human rights watchdog organization—reports that human rights abuses are still prevalent in Africa. According to the organization's 2007 report (which reports on 2006 events), from which the viewpoint is excerpted, African governments are still rife with corruption, thwarting political and economic progress. Many governments are run by dictators, and Amnesty International states that these autocratic regimes have used arrests, harassment, and election-rigging to remain in control. The organization also notes that conflicts still rage across the continent, displacing populations and creating a pretext for other human rights violations such as rape, murder, and looting. Amnesty International blames much of the abuses on weak national and international institutions that lack the strength or resolve to stand up to the warlords and tyrants who hold power.

Amnesty International, *Amnesty International Report 2007: The State of the World's Human Rights.* UK: Alden, 2007.

As you read, consider the following questions:

1. In Amnesty International's view, why have the 2006 elections in the Democratic Republic of the Congo failed to bring about peace in that nation?

2. As the author relates, how have the governments of Eritrea, Ethiopia, Rwanda, and other African nations impinged on journalists' right to free expression?

3. Why are women and girls in African nations such as South Africa and Swaziland at a higher risk of contracting AIDS and of not receiving treatment for the disease, according to Amnesty International?

The human rights situation in many parts of Africa remained precarious in 2006. Armed conflict, underdevelopment, extreme poverty, widespread corruption, inequitable distribution of resources, political repression, marginalization, ethnic and civil violence, and the HIV/AIDS pandemic continued to undermine the enjoyment of human rights across the region.

Although armed conflicts generally were on the decrease, they still affected many countries. As a result, several million refugees and internally displaced people, including children and the elderly, remained without basic shelter, protection and care.

Most states suppressed dissent and the free expression of opinion. Some governments authorized or condoned extrajudicial execution, arbitrary arrests, torture and other ill-treatment, or harassment of opposition political activists, human rights defenders and journalists. Across the region, suspects in criminal investigations continued to be at high risk of torture in part because of poor police training and supervision, as well as public pressure on police to tackle high rates of crime.

The enjoyment of economic, social and cultural rights such as the rights to food, shelter, health and education remained a mere illusion for the vast majority of people in Africa. Corruption and under-investment in social services contributed to entrenched poverty.

Armed Conflicts

At least a dozen countries in Africa were affected by armed conflict. Marginalization of certain communities, small arms proliferation and struggles for geo-political power and control of natural resources were some of the underlying causes of the conflicts.

Although there were numerous peace and international mediation processes, Burundi, Central African Republic (CAR), Chad, Côte d'Ivoire, Democratic Republic of the Congo (DRC), Eritrea, Ethiopia, the Republic of Congo, Senegal, Sudan and Somalia were among the countries still engaged in or affected by conflict. In all these countries, civilians continued to suffer human rights abuses, and the most affected were women, children and the elderly. The conflicts in CAR, Chad, Sudan and Somalia (with the involvement of Ethiopia), represented an escalation of conflict in central and east Africa.

Even in countries where peace processes were under way, such as in Côte d'Ivoire, the DRC and Sudan, civilians continued to face attacks and were inadequately protected by their governments.

Conflict continued in the Darfur region of Sudan, despite the Darfur Peace Agreement. The Sudanese government failed to disarm the armed militia known as the Janjawid, which attacked civilians in Sudan and eastern Chad. Tens of thousands of Darfuris who escaped the killing, rape and pillage were living in refugee camps in CAR and Chad, unable to return to their villages. At least 200,000 people had died and 2.5 million internally displaced by the end of 2006.

Armed opposition groups in Chad, Côte d'Ivoire and Sudan carried out human rights abuses, and in CAR, Chad and Sudan they continued to launch attacks against their respective government forces using other countries as bases.

Despite presidential and legislative elections in the DRC, the peace process and future stability of the country remained under serious threat, particularly because of the failure to reform the new national army into a professional and apolitical force that respects human rights. The new army committed numerous serious human rights violations and the government failed to exclude suspected perpetrators from its ranks. Congolese armed groups, as well as foreign armed groups from Burundi, Rwanda and Uganda present in the DRC, also threatened the peace and committed human rights abuses. Lack of security limited humanitarian access to many areas in the east.

Proliferation of small arms remained a serious problem, particularly in Burundi, the DRC, Somalia and Sudan, contributing to a vicious cycle of violence, instability, poor human rights situations and humanitarian crises.

In Angola, the Memorandum of Understanding for Peace and Reconciliation in Cabinda was signed by the government and the Cabindan Forum for Dialogue, formally ending the armed conflict in Cabinda. However, sporadic attacks by both sides against civilians persisted.

Despite intense diplomatic efforts, notably by the UN and the African Union (AU), human rights abuses continued to be reported in Côte d'Ivoire. Government security forces and the Forces Nouvelles (New Forces), a coalition of armed groups in control of the north since September 2002, were implicated. Both protagonists repeatedly postponed disarmament and demobilization, and the reintegration programme remained deadlocked because of disagreement over the timetable.

In Somalia, the militias of the Union of Islamic Courts, which had conquered Mogadishu, were defeated [six months later] by an Ethiopian force supporting the internationally recognized Transitional Federal Government. Uncertainties remained about the deployment of an AU peace support force to protect this government, as authorized by the UN Security Council.

The border dispute between Ethiopia and Eritrea continued to be a source of tension.

Economic, Social and Cultural Rights

The realization of economic, social and cultural rights remained illusory in virtually all countries in Africa. Struggling economies, under-development, under-investment in basic social services, corruption, and marginalization of certain communities were some of the factors behind the failure to realise these basic human rights. In countries such as Angola, Chad, the DRC, Equatorial Guinea, Nigeria, the Republic of Congo and Sudan, the presence of oil and other minerals continued to blight rather than enhance people's lives because of conflicts, corruption and power struggles.

Hundreds of thousands of people in many African countries were deliberately rendered homeless. By forcibly evicting people without due process of law, adequate compensation or provision of alternative shelter, governments violated people's internationally recognized human right to shelter and adequate housing.

Such evictions, which were often accompanied by disproportionate use of force and other abuses, were known to have taken place in Angola, Equatorial Guinea, Kenya, Nigeria and Sudan. In one incident, bulldozers arrived unannounced in Dar al-Salam, a settlement for displaced people 43 kilometres south of Khartoum, Sudan, and began demolishing the homes of some 12,000 people, many of whom had fled drought, famine, the north-south civil war and, most recently, the conflict in Darfur. Some 50,000 other people in Sudan continued to face eviction as a result of the building of the Meroe dam; in

2006 a total of 2,723 households in the Amri area were given six days to evacuate their homes and reportedly given no shelter, food or medicine.

The HIV/AIDS pandemic continued to pose a threat to millions of Africans. According to UNAIDS (the Joint UN Programme on HIV/AIDS), the virus caused 2.1 million deaths in 2006 and 2.8 million people were newly infected, bringing to 24.7 million the total number of people living with HIV/AIDS on the continent.

Women and girls in Africa remained 40 per cent more likely to be infected with the virus than men, and often carried the main burden as carers. Violence against women and girls in some countries also increased their risk of HIV infection.

National responses to HIV/AIDS continued to be scaled up throughout the continent. The roll-out of anti-retroviral treatment continued, albeit unevenly. In June UNAIDS estimated that more than one million people on the continent were receiving life-saving anti-retroviral therapy—23 per cent of those who required it.

In South Africa, the country with the largest number of people living with HIV/AIDS, the government showed signs of greater openness to the participation of civil society organizations in achieving a more effective response to the pandemic.

At the AU Special Summit on HIV/AIDS, Tuberculosis and Malaria in Abuja, Nigeria, in May, African governments commited themselves to "universal access to treatment, care and prevention services for all people by 2010." This call was reiterated, albeit with few tangible commitments, at the UN General Assembly High Level Review Meeting on HIV/AIDs (UNGASS Review) shortly afterwards. UN member states committed themselves to working towards achieving universal access to treatment, care and prevention by 2010. Countries throughout the region were developing national targets and indicators for achieving this aim.

Tuberculosis and malaria also posed a serious threat in many areas. In 2006 tuberculosis killed over 500,000 people across the region and around 900,000 people in Africa, most of them young children, died from acute cases of malaria.

Repression of Dissent

Repression of dissent continued in many countries. The authorities in Eritrea, Ethiopia, Rwanda, Sudan, Uganda and Zimbabwe were among those that used a licensing/accreditation system to restrict the work of journalists and consequently impinged on the freedom of expression. The promulgation and use of anti-terror and public order laws to restrict dissent and the work of human rights defenders continued in some states, and human rights defenders were particularly vulnerable in Burundi, the DRC, Ethiopia, Rwanda, Somalia, Sudan and Zimbabwe.

In Ethiopia, for example, opposition party leaders, journalists and human rights defenders who were prisoners of conscience were tried on capital charges such as treason, attempted genocide and armed conspiracy. In Eritrea, members of minority evangelical churches were imprisoned because of their faith, and former government leaders, members of parliament and journalists continued to be held without trial, many of them feared dead.

Death Penalty

The death penalty continued to be widely applied and prisoners remained under sentence of death in several countries in the region, including around 600 people in Rwanda. However, the Tanzanian authorities commuted all death sentences during 2006, and the ruling party in Rwanda recommended abolition of capital punishment.

In the DRC, military tribunals continued to pass the death penalty after unfair trials, although there were no reports of state executions. In Equatorial Guinea, one person was publicly executed for murder.

Impunity

Police officers and other law enforcement personnel in many parts of the region continued to commit human rights violations, including unlawful killings, torture or other ill-treatment, with impunity. However, there were important developments in the efforts to end impunity for war crimes and other serious crimes under international law.

Following the referral of the situation in Darfur by the UN Security Council in March 2005, the Office of the Prosecutor of the International Criminal Court (ICC) visited Khartoum in 2006.

Warrants of arrest issued in 2005 against senior members of the Ugandan armed political group, the Lord's Resistance Army (LRA)—including Joseph Kony, Vincent Otti, Okot

Odhiambo and Dominic Ongwen—remained in force, but the accused were not apprehended. The LRA leaders argued that the warrants should be withdrawn before they would commit to a peace agreement, but the warrants remained in force at the end of the year.

In the DRC, Thomas Lubanga Dyilo, leader of an Ituri armed group, the Union of Congolese Patriots, was arrested and charged with war crimes—specifically, recruiting and using in hostilities children aged under 15. He was subsequently transferred to the ICC in The Hague, the Netherlands.

In March, former Liberian President Charles Taylor was handed over to Liberia by Nigeria, where he had been living. He was then transferred to the Special Court for Sierra Leone to face trial on charges of war crimes and crimes against humanity committed during the armed conflict in Sierra Leone. In addition, three trials before the Special Court continued of those bearing the greatest responsibility for crimes against humanity, war crimes and other serious violations of international law committed in the civil war in Sierra Leone after 30 November 1996.

In Ethiopia, the 12-year trial of former President Mengistu Hailemariam ended in December with his conviction for genocide, mass killings and other crimes. Along with 24 other members of the Dergue military government (1974–1991), he was tried in his absence while in exile in Zimbabwe. Zimbabwe President Robert Mugabe had refused to extradite him for trial.

In July 2006, the AU Assembly of Heads of State and Government asked Senegal to try Hissène Habré, Chad's former President, for crimes against humanity he committed while in power (1982–1990). He had been living in Senegal since he was ousted from office. In 2005 a Belgian judge issued an international arrest warrant for torture and other crimes committed during his rule. In November 2006 Senegal's Council of Ministers adopted a draft law allowing Hissène Habré to be tried.

Trials of prominent genocide suspects continued before the International Criminal Tribunal for Rwanda (ICTR), which held 57 detainees at the end of 2006. Ten trials were ongoing. The UN Security Council asked the ICTR to complete all trials by the end of 2008. However, the ICTR failed to indict or prosecute leaders of the former Rwandese Patriotic Front widely believed to have authorized, condoned or carried out war crimes and crimes against humanity in 1994.

In Rwanda, concerns remained about the impartiality and fairness of gacaca tribunals (a community-based system of tribunals established in Rwanda in 2002 to try people suspected of crimes during the 1994 genocide).

Violence Against Women and Girls

Violence against women and girls remained pervasive and only a few countries were considering laws to address the problem. Parliaments in Kenya, Nigeria, South Africa and Zimbabwe continued to discuss draft legislation on domestic violence and sexual offences.

In South Africa and Swaziland in particular, the pervasiveness of gender-based violence continued to place women and girls at risk of HIV/AIDS directly or through obstructing their access to information, prevention and treatment. Gender-based violence, as well as stigma and discrimination, also affected access to treatment for those already living with HIV/AIDS.

The practice of female genital mutilation remained widespread in some countries, particularly Sierra Leone, Somalia and Sudan.

In the DRC, women and girls were raped by government security forces and armed groups and had little or no access to adequate medical treatment. In Darfur, rape of women by

Janjawid militias continued to be systematic. The number of women attacked and raped while searching for firewood around Kalma Camp near Nyala, South Darfur, increased from about three or four a month to some 200 a month between June and August.

In Nigeria there were frequent reports of sexual violence, including rape, by state officials. Such abuses were committed with impunity. In Côte d'Ivoire there were continuing reports of sexual violence against women in the government-controlled areas and the region held by Forces Nouvelles.

Regional Institutions and Human Rights

Although the Constitutive Act of the AU underscores the centrality of the promotion and protection of human rights throughout the continent, the AU fell short of its commitment to human rights generally. The AU continued to demonstrate a deep reluctance to publicly criticize African leaders who failed to protect human rights, especially in Sudan and Zimbabwe.

A combination of lack of political will and capacity of the AU to halt continuing conflicts in places such as Darfur, and the apathy of an international community that had the capacity but lacked the will to act, left millions of civilians at the mercy of belligerent governments and ruthless warlords.

Many of the institutions referred to under the Constitutive Act of the AU became fully operational in 2006 but they made little or no impact on people's lives. However, the election of 11 judges to the newly established African Court on Human and Peoples' Rights enhanced the prospects of developing a culture that would respect the rule of law and human rights regionally. The Court held its first meeting in July and the judges began drafting the Court's rules of procedure. A draft legal instrument relating to the establishment of a merged court comprising the African Court on Human and Peoples' Rights and the African Court of Justice was being negotiated at the end of the year.

The African Peer Review Mechanism completed the review of Ghana, Rwanda and South Africa but failed to make its findings public. The African Commission on Human and Peoples' Rights, which remained the only functional regional human rights body, continued to be denied the much needed human, material and financial resources to fully respond to the many human rights problems in the region.

Overall, widespread and massive corruption in Africa continued to contribute to a vicious cycle of extreme poverty, manifesting itself in violations of internationally recognized human rights, especially economic and social rights, weak institutions and leadership, and marginalization of the most vulnerable sectors of the population, including women and children.

> *"Africa's progress disproves the distorted and widespread portrayal of the continent as a sea of conflict and undifferentiated poverty."*

Africa Is Making Improvements in Human Rights

Asha-Rose Migiro

The following viewpoint is a speech Asha-Rose Migiro, the deputy secretary-general of the United Nations, presented to the New York City Bar Association Committee on African Affairs. In the viewpoint, Migiro argues that the state of affairs in Africa is not as dreary as the media often portray. She states that the number of conflicts in Africa is decreasing while African leaders are increasingly engaging in peace talks. Free elections have been held in some troubled nations, and international organizations have become instrumental in challenging human rights abuses, Migiro contends. In addition, she notes, education opportunities have improved, and countries are making progress toward alleviating poverty. Migiro was the foreign minister of Tanzania before assuming the UN post.

Asha-Rose Migiro, Press Release: Remarks of Deputy Secretary-General at New York City Bar Association Committee on African Affairs in New York, June 6, 2007. Reprinted with the permission of the United Nations.

As you read, consider the following questions:

1. What does Migiro say has been a positive result of peace talks between the government of Uganda and the Lord's Resistance Army?

2. According to the author, what percentage of the population of the Democratic Republic of the Congo turned out to vote in the 2006 elections?

3. How many African nations have achieved economic growth rates of more than 5 percent since the late 1990s, according to Migiro?

G atherings such as these are a demonstration of crucial support to the United Nations. I am, therefore, delighted to join all of you today to discuss a topic that is always at the top of the United Nations' agenda—the challenges affecting Africa.

As enlightened friends of Africa, you know that the reality is vastly different from the image sometimes conveyed by the media. You know that Africa's progress disproves the distorted and widespread portrayal of the continent as a sea of conflict and undifferentiated poverty.

Violent Conflict Is Diminishing

Compared to a decade ago, the number of violent conflicts has dropped dramatically. Africans are increasingly taking ownership of the security agenda. In many parts of the continent, remarkable advances have been made in ending armed conflict and consolidating peace.

Burundi and Sierra Leone are two fine examples. After the successful conclusion of peacekeeping mandates, the UN is working closely with these countries to help shape a better future. And the United Nations Peacebuilding Commission is contributing to these efforts. Liberia is another success story. A landmark vote there [in 2005] brought into office the first woman ever to be elected President of an African State.

More recently, direct talks between the Government of Uganda and the leaders of the Lord's Resistance Army [LRA, a rebel group] have renewed hopes that the horrible conflict affecting northern Uganda for the past 20 years will finally be brought to an end. The talks have already led to an improved security situation in northern Uganda, leading some internally displaced people to start returning to their home areas. The Special Envoy of the UN Secretary-General for LRA-Affected Areas, former Mozambican President Joachim Chissano, is playing an important role in supporting these peace efforts.

The peace process for Côte d'Ivoire has also witnessed positive developments of late. The Ivorian parties have made a good start in implementing the Agreement they signed in Ouagadougou in March [2007], creating a real opportunity for a peaceful solution to the crisis.

The Democratic Republic of the Congo provides an even more remarkable example of progress towards post-conflict recovery and democratic governance. [In 2006], the UN worked with the African Union and other partners to support the Congolese people in holding the first free elections in more than 40 years. This endeavour was achieved with the support of a UN peacekeeping operation. It also benefited from the largest electoral support engagement in UN history. Above all, it was testimony to the courage and determination of the Congolese people. Seventy per cent of the electorate turned out to cast their vote in a calm and peaceful ballot.

And yet, as you know all too well, violence continues to have tragic consequences for civilians in Africa's remaining conflict areas. Nowhere is the tragedy of conflict more evident than in Darfur [in Sudan]. Despite the joint efforts of the UN and the African Union to reinvigorate the peace process and strengthen peacekeeping, the violence there is taking an unacceptable toll on human lives.

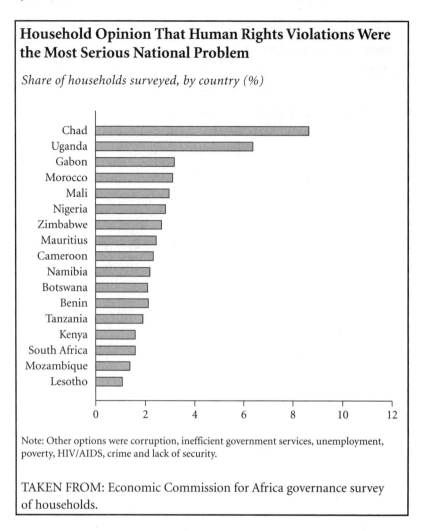

Household Opinion That Human Rights Violations Were the Most Serious National Problem

Share of households surveyed, by country (%)

Note: Other options were corruption, inefficient government services, unemployment, poverty, HIV/AIDS, crime and lack of security.

TAKEN FROM: Economic Commission for Africa governance survey of households.

Peacekeeping in Darfur

Today, there is no single issue to which the Secretary-General or his senior colleagues devote more efforts than Darfur. The United Nations has organized what is currently its largest humanitarian operation in the world. We are engaging politically at numerous levels with the Government of Sudan, the Darfurian factions, countries in the region, organizations such as the African Union, and key world powers. The goal is to work out a negotiated solution and deploy a robust peacekeeping operation capable of supporting an enhanced peace agreement.

Recently, the Government of Sudan confirmed its agreement on the entire heavy support package of the United Nations assistance to the African Union Mission in Sudan. I am encouraged by this development. We intend to move quickly with the deployment, in close cooperation with the African Union.

Member States of the United Nations agree that the three pillars of our work—development, security and human rights—are not only vitally important in their own right; they reinforce—indeed, depend on—each other.

So as we strive to resolve conflicts and build peace, we must devote equal energy to promoting human rights and the rule of law. I know this is an area of particular interest to your Committee on African Affairs. And I commend you for your commitment to strengthening the rule of law and the administration of justice in Africa. So much needs to be done before we can speak of a real improvement in Africa's human rights situation.

Monitoring Human Rights

It will be recalled that, at the 2005 World Summit, all the world's Governments agreed in principle to the responsibility to protect: to act collectively, through the Security Council, when a population is threatened with genocide, ethnic cleansing, or crimes against humanity. Our challenge now is to give real meaning to the concept, by taking steps to make it operational.

[In late April 2007], the Secretary-General appointed Francis Deng of Sudan as his new Special Adviser for the Prevention of Genocide and Mass Atrocities. A distinguished expert in human rights and international law, Mr. Deng joins us from the United States Institute of Peace, the Massachusetts

Institute of Technology and Johns Hopkins University. He will devote himself full-time to his mission with the United Nations.

As you know, we also have a new intergovernmental instrument charged with upholding human rights. The members of the UN Human Rights Council are tasked with working together to promote an objective and universal approach. Council members should also use every mechanism at their disposal—from the help of independent experts to universal periodic review—to advance the cause of human rights. I remain hopeful that all victims of human rights abuses will be able to look to the Human Rights Council as a forum and a springboard for action.

Tackling Poverty and Bettering Education

We must also devote equal efforts to eradicating extreme poverty and improving living conditions and livelihoods in Africa. [The year 2007] will have to see real movement towards the Millennium Development Goals [international plan to reduce poverty and other social ills], our common vision for a better world by 2015. Midway towards that date, we have arrived at a tipping point.

Many countries in Africa have made good progress towards reaching the Millennium Development Goals. Since the late 1990s, more than a dozen African nations have achieved average growth rates of above 5 per cent. Many low-income countries have lifted sizeable proportions of their citizens above the poverty line. Several are on course to meet the target of halving poverty by 2015.

Around 15 African countries have already achieved universal primary education, or are on track to do so. And most Southern African countries are on course to attain gender parity at the primary school level.

Work to Be Done

However, we face enormous challenges in meeting some of the Goals. Overall, the number of people living in extreme poverty in Africa is rising. And child mortality rates remain very high. The world needs to focus on accelerating implementation of existing commitments to achieve the Goals. Concerted action now—on poverty, on health and HIV/AIDS, on education and on other needs—may mean the difference between success and failure in achieving these crucial targets. This in turn will mean the difference between life and death for millions of Africans.

Civil society and professional organizations such as yours have a vital role to play in all three pillars of our work—development, security and human rights. Given the many pressing challenges on our agenda, your support is indispensable. I am grateful to you for your commitment.

Periodical Bibliography

The following articles have been selected to supplement the diverse views presented in this chapter.

Baffour Ankomah — "There Is Hope for Africa" *New African*, June 2007.

William F. Buckley Jr. — "Superstitions of Democracy," *National Review*, May 28, 2007.

Pusch Coomey — "South Africa: To BEE or Not to BEE," *New African*, August-September 2007.

Economist — "Will Africa Ever Get It Right?" April 28, 2007.

William Gumede — "Nobody Does It Worse," *New Statesman*, June 26, 2006.

Joshua Hammer — "Freedom Is Not Enough," *Newsweek*, November 14, 2005.

David Hollenbach — "More Than One Way of Dying," *America*, January 15, 2007.

Tanangachi Mfuni — "Grandad Reide Challenges Child Labor in Africa," *Amsterdam (NY) News*, September 7, 2006.

Dismas Nkunda — "An African Struggle," *New Internationalist*, June 2007.

Lydia Polgreen — "Africa's Crisis of Democracy," *New York Times*, April 23, 2007.

Lydia Polgreen — "A Country and a Continent, Hanging in the Balance," *New York Times*, January 23, 2006.

Alec Russell — "Exodus from Poverty and Terror," *New Statesman*, April 2, 2007.

Harold Smith — "How Britain Undermined Democracy in Africa," *New African*, May 2005.

How Can the West Help Bring Peace to Africa?

Chapter Preface

In a 2007 report for TomPaine.com, a progressive online news journal, Eric Nicholls, a researcher for the Human Security Centre at the University of British Columbia, writes that sub-Saharan Africa is more peaceful today than it has been in the past forty years. As he notes, in 1999 there were sixteen wars ravaging sub-Saharan states; by 2005, the number had fallen to five. "Increased peacemaking, peacekeeping and peacebuilding activities deserve much of the credit," Nicholls asserts.

Although Nicholls credits African governments with taking steps to bring about peace in the region, he maintains that international efforts—primarily orchestrated by the United Nations—had much to do with conflict reduction. Peacekeeping missions run by the UN are present in eight sub-Saharan countries, while various European Union troops are stationed in other regional hotspots. Perhaps the most significant deployment in recent years is the up to twenty-six thousand African Union and UN troops slated to patrol the Darfur area of Sudan where fighting between government-backed militias and local rebel groups have claimed two hundred thousand lives since 2003.

Peacekeeping missions in Africa have traditionally been staffed by African soldiers but paid for by American and European money. Some believe that the dominance of African troops is appropriate because the nations that supply the soldiers often have a vested interest in quelling regional conflicts before they can spread instability to neighboring states. Critics, however, have noted reluctance on the part of some Western powers—and the United States in particular—to send soldiers into Africa, fearing the type of nose-bloodying that the U.S. military received after intervening in the Somalia crisis in 1993. To take up the slack on behalf of Western nations, various American and European private military contractors have been engaged by the UN to train, lead, or simply support African peacekeeping forces.

While the United States has refrained from sending troops to Africa on peacekeeping missions, it has beefed up its support of counterterrorism measures on the continent. Though again not committing significant manpower to the project, the U.S. government is instead increasing funding to the cause. In 2003, President George W. Bush launched the $100 million East Africa Counterterrorism Initiative (EACTI) that seeks to improve intergovernmental communications and pays for the training of port security and border patrol units in various African states. Other recent initiatives are funding the development and training of police forces in countries such as Tanzania, Uganda, and Ethiopia. Champions of these policies contend that counterterrorism efforts are a form of peacekeeping because they help defeat extremists who often incite civil wars as well as fan the flames of anti-American sentiment. Critics, however, complain that these initiatives are merely examples of U.S. self-interest and a lack of resolve to bring peace to a continent where high death tolls and refugee crises are of little concern to America's agenda.

The viewpoints composing the following chapter examine the effectiveness of Western peacekeeping efforts in Africa. Most call upon the United States and the international community to take a firmer hand in ending African conflicts; others suggest that increased involvement may exacerbate regional tensions.

> "An important element of this campaign
> of intimidation, depopulation and
> murder has been the use of sexual vio-
> lence."

The West Should Support Prosecution of War Crimes in Darfur

Brian Brivati

*In the following viewpoint, Brian Brivati describes the conflict
over land and resources in Darfur, Sudan, between the
government-backed Janjaweed militias and rebel groups tied to
the black populations in the region. The refugees in Darfur are
the ones who suffer the tragedies of displacement, rape, and
murder, and who want those responsible for such war crimes
brought to justice. Brian Brivati teaches genocide studies at
Kingston University in London and writes for the* New Statesman *news magazine.*

As you read, consider the following questions:

1. According to Brivati, how many ethnic Africans have
   been killed in the past two years in the Darfur region?

2. What, in the author's opinion, is the real reason that genocide takes place?

3. According to Brivati, what is the solution for the problems facing Darfur?

A humanitarian disaster is unfolding right now in the Darfur region of Sudan, and it could be prevented. More than 300,000 people, most of them ethnically African, have been killed in the past two years [2005–2007]. Some 3.3 million have been forced to flee into camps as a campaign of terror by Janjaweed militias and the army of the government of Sudan clears large areas of the region. The campaign is co-ordinated and systematic. NGOs [nongovernmental organizations] that hope to give limited help are themselves subject to intimidation. The latest reports suggest that up to 40 per cent of those designated ethnically African cannot be protected.

Rebels fighting the government have also attacked camps and killed civilians. There is, however, an utter disparity in power and violence perpetrated, between the rebel groups and the government/Janjaweed forces. Moreover, the government deploys an overtly Arab-supremacist ideology, chillingly expressed in Janjaweed chants of "Kill the blacks, kill the slaves", and evidence exists of written orders from the government "to change the demography of Darfur and empty it of African tribes".

An important element of this campaign of intimidation, depopulation and murder has been the use of sexual violence. [In December 2006] Amnesty International reported on a "dramatic increase in the numbers of rapes" in Darfur. Amnesty, Unicef, the Aegis Trust and other groups that take a range of views on the conflict all agree that sexual violence is central and systematic to this conflict.

Ongoing Violence Against a Culture

There are few cases of straightforward genocide in which a dominant state sets out to annihilate an ethnic group because of *who* they are (rather than what they do or think). The Nazis arguably did so against the Jews; Rwanda's Hutu *génocidaires* did so against the Tutsis. But there are many more cases in which mass killing escalates out of intra-state conflicts that spill over into other states. There are two things that set these kinds of cases apart from "ordinary" civil wars. The first is the killing of significant numbers of civilians because of identities projected on to them. The second is that these projected identifies determine who lives and who dies. The killing becomes the purpose of the project: civilians are killed not for a piece of land or other resources, but because of who they are. This kind of killing creates a cycle in which victims then kill for reasons equally meaningless strategically or economically. Such reprisals lead people to question the use of the word *genocide*.

As in Rwanda, there has been an unconstructive debate about the appropriateness of the term in Darfur. We seem to be frightened of seeing genocide as something distinctive; the debate becomes a word game—is this conflict genocide or is it not? Rather than becoming trapped in semantics, however, we ought to focus on how state-sponsored mass murder acquires a dynamic of its own.

The Fate of Darfur

Darfur and Sudan more generally, was for 200 years a victim of both Egyptian and British imperialism. Then, for generations, the region was neglected by the central government of Sudan. The Sudan Political Service, which governed the area during colonial rule by the British, treated Darfur as a little piece of "authentic" Africa in which it could play king. This institutional condescension created a template of indifference with which post-independence governments in Darfur have continued to operate. In the hands of the post-colonial ruling elite, this template was given an Arab-supremacist inflection that then became an ideology of mass murder. The 1984–85 famine showed the world the extent of central government indifference to the fate of Darfur.

During Sudan's long civil war, the Darfur region was further isolated. When the Comprehensive Peace Agreement was signed in January 2005, a quick Darfur Peace Agreement was also put in place, but it did nothing to meet the needs and demands of the people of Darfur.

How can the "international community" respond to crimes against humanity that are products of post-colonial politics and ideologies but also rooted in imperial legacies? First, we should admit that we are not an international community but a set of competing interest groups. In a unipolar world governed by the United States, it has been in the interests of some groups to pretend that intervention to prevent crimes against humanity or genocide is impossible.

But this is simply not true: China and other states have protected the Khartoum government while the US has been powerless to act. The reality is that Washington could do nothing to stop any state acting unilaterally to stop this killing, and would actually welcome anyone doing so.

Mesmerised by US history and by post-invasion Iraq, the international human-rights industry has also been slow to state what is now obvious. This is not an American problem. This is not a British problem. This is not even an EU [European Union] problem. None of them could take the lead in solving it. This is an African, Arab and Asian problem. The solution is not invasion, or occupation, or regime change. The solution is in the hands of China and the African, Arab and other Asian states that surround, trade with and finance Sudan.

No-Fly Zone

What could these states or groups of states do? Khartoum has been persuaded to accept the deployment of a limited hybrid force. The first part of a UN force, comprising 43 military staff officers and 24 policemen, arrived in Sudan on 28 December [2006]: this deployment must now be built upon in various ways. First, the initial deployment of UN troops in Darfur should be hugely speeded up and extended. Second, a UN resolution should authorise the imposition of a no-fly zone over western Darfur to protect the camps of internally displaced people.

The government in Khartoum should accept both of these actions by acknowledging that it is no longer in control of the situation and that it requires help to protect aid supplies. But it should be made clear that both interventions will be non-consensual if necessary. President Omar el-Bashir's government has taken a series of gambles on the indifference of the world to the fate of Darfur's people, and he will continue to do so. At the same time he cannily presents Sudan as an Islamic state that is the victim of imperialist intervention in search of oil. It isn't, and the imperial power chasing oil hardest in Sudan at this moment is communist China.

There is a simple enough response to this charade. The deployment should be made up from Asian, African and Arab states and the regional organisations representing these states should make it clear that the government of Sudan will be completely isolated unless it moves to control the Janjaweed. Equal pressure must be put on states and groups currently supporting the rebels, especially Chad. The role of the west and nations that trade with Sudan—for example, Japan, China and Malaysia—is to bring economic pressure to bear on the Sudanese government and to offer economic incentives.

The Need for Peace in Darfur

It is clear what needs to be done to bring peace to Darfur. But will it happen? A humanitarian disaster is unfolding before our eyes and cannot be prevented. A hybrid force may gradually be deployed over the next eight or nine months, by which time many thousands will have died and the government and rebels alike will have become radicalised by each other's actions. The fighting will continue to spill into neighbouring states. The civil war in Sudan between north and south may start again. But the long-term consequences of Darfur will go far beyond these terrible possibilities. They will be profound for the system of international relations in the post-Iraq-war world and they will seriously challenge European ideas of the universalism of human rights. This universalism holds that there are some things that all human beings should enjoy and some things no human being should endure.

Western imperialism can be blamed for many things, but there is no imperialist explanation for why African, Asian and Arab states do not act over Darfur. They face no logistical obstacle to establishing a no-fly zone. The problem is one of will, not agency or capability.

What ought to unite us against genocide is that, in the end, there is no conceivable geopolitical gain to be had from working with genocidal regimes. The path they have embarked upon has no strategic dimension and it will, in time, self-destruct. These are allies you do not wish to have, neighbours you cannot trust, crimes you cannot live with.

| "There is inherent conflict in trying to deliver justice in an area without peace."

War-Crime Prosecutions Will Not Bring Peace to Darfur

Anja Tranovich

In the following viewpoint, Anja Tranovich states that the International Criminal Court (ICC) has a difficult job in bringing justice to war criminals in Darfur, Sudan, where a conflict between anti-government rebels and mercenary Janjaweed militia units has claimed many lives and forced people to flee their homes. Tranovich contends that the ICC has no muscle to deliver warrants and arrest suspects without international aid, which the United Nations seems unwilling to give. Tranovich also worries that ICC investigations would lead to more violence, as the Sudanese government has taken an aggressive stance against foreign interference in a civil war.

As you read, consider the following questions:

1. As Tranovich reports, how was news of the government's alliance with the Janjaweed militias leaked in Sudan?

Anja Tranovich, "Seeking Justice Where There Is No Peace," *Nation*, May 24, 2006. Reproduced by permission.

2. Why does Eric Reeves—as quoted by the author—argue that progress in ICC trials will not likely end the violence in Darfur?

3. Why does Tranovich state that the ICC "cannot fulfill its mandate with visibility"?

On March 31, 2005, the UN Security Council voted to refer the ongoing atrocities in Darfur to the International Criminal Court (ICC), which was created in 1998 to prosecute the gravest international crimes. That evening the ICC, which had not yet held a trial, was handed a genocidal quagmire, a hostile government and a near-mandate to prosecute.

International trials conducted in public seek to repair the power imbalance between criminal and victim and are a visible reactivation and reassurance of justice. The ICC hopes to achieve this in Sudan. But the new court is untested; no one knows how the trials will affect complex political situations like the one unfolding in Darfur.

The ICC's first year in operation has shown that pursuing justice does not always create peace. Deirdre Clancy, a coordinator of the Darfur Consortium, put it this way: "The ICC is a huge idea and has a huge potential to have an impact, but it's a bunch of lawyers in The Hague [Netherlands] negotiating an extraordinarily complicated situation with security problems" and without much international help.

The first meetings of the ICC took place some five years before the Security Council referral. One hundred sixty countries, including Sudan, participated in creating the ICC framework. The court has a mandate to bring to trial heads of states and others who have committed crimes against humanity, genocide and war crimes. It is designed to prosecute only when state courts cannot or will not. It seeks to try those responsible for the Rwandas or Holocausts of the future and, by ensuring accountability, to deter them from happening altogether.

In 1997 UN Secretary General Kofi Annan made this lofty and much-repeated statement about the ICC: "In the prospect of an international criminal court lies the promise of universal justice. That is the simple and soaring hope of this vision ... to ensure that no ruler, no State, no junta [military rule] and no army anywhere can abuse human rights with impunity. Only then will the innocents of distant wars and conflicts know that they, too, may sleep under the cover of justice, that they, too, have rights, and that those who violate those rights will be punished."

The Complex Problem in Darfur

In the context of a strong statute and widespread international support, many believed Annan's "never again" was coming to fruition. By the March 2005 referral, the Darfur conflict had been declared a genocide by the President of the United States, presidential hopeful John Kerry, then-Secretary of State Colin Powell and the entire US Congress. The UN described the conflict as "the world's worst humanitarian crisis."

The largest country in Africa, Sudan is comparable in size to the United States east of the Mississippi. Its regions have never been united within the colonial boundaries inherited from Egypt and England by its first Arab leaders in 1957. The country has been at civil war for all but about a decade of its existence, largely because wealth and power are disproportionately focused in the Arab-dominated central region. When an armed resistance movement surfaced in Darfur in 2003, a long-neglected region in the West, the central government struck back hard. It solicited and armed a local nomadic group ethnically tied to the Arab government to fight the rebels and, by association, the local Fur population. The Arab fighters became known as Janjaweed. Alex de Waal, a consultant to the Darfur peace negotiations, described the conflict as a "counterinsurgency on the cheap." A military memo leaked to Sudan Radio Service gave the Janjaweed orders to kill all Fur leaders, representatives and intellectuals and to use all means possible to capture Fur cattle, donkeys and horses. The memo spelled out a plan aimed at eliminating "black tribes" from the region. An estimated 450,000 people have died in Darfur, and more than 2 million, one-third of Darfur's entire population, have been displaced.

De Waal noted that the systematic scorched-earth campaigns, murders and rapes of the people in Darfur are grossly disproportionate to the military threat of the rebellion. They are the deliberate destruction of a community. "This is the routine cruelty of a security cabal, its humanity withered by years in power: it is genocide by force of habit," he wrote in *The London Review of Books*.

Some progress has been made to resolve the conflict. One of the rebel groups recently signed a peace deal with the Khartoum central government. However, Eric Reeves, an American academic who has written extensively on the region, noted that this agreement is only as good as the progress Khartoum makes meeting the various benchmarks in the deal. The government has systematically failed the standards of all previous peace agreements and ceasefires. "There is rampant bad faith," he said in an interview. There is also still violence on the ground. A recently proposed UN peacekeeping mission would take at least six months to get into Sudan, if it gets there at all. Khartoum has not yet said it will allow such a mission, and the resolution the Security Council just passed only authorizes an assessment for a peace mission, not the intervention itself. Reeves noted that any intervention would need a mandate to use force in order to be effective against the Janjaweed.

The Precarious Position of the ICC

The ICC was created to prosecute crimes such as those taking place in Darfur, but building criminal cases amid ongoing violence is a daunting challenge. There is inherent conflict in trying to deliver justice in an area without peace; prioritizing either peace or justice poses political choices no one wants to make. The stakes for the new court are high.

"Most people here realize we are now under a magnifying glass," an ICC official recently told a *New York Times* reporter. "It could make or break the institution."

The ICC was never intended to operate in isolation. International forces serve arrest warrants, and ICC personnel need access to the conflicted country to gather evidence. No ICC investigators have thus far entered Sudan—the government won't permit it. ICC prosecutor Luis Moreno-Ocampo told the United Nations General Assembly that "continuing insecurities in Darfur did not allow for an effective system of victim and witness protection." This has forced his office to collect evidence and interview witnesses outside of Sudan and "is a serious impediment in effective investigations." The ICC is still in its evidence-gathering phase and struggling against a hostile government. Mere discussion of the ICC cannot happen openly in Sudan for fear of government repression.

One of the problems the ICC faces is that it relies on pressure from the international community to help bring perpetrators of crimes against humanity to justice. The government in Khartoum won't cooperate with the ICC unless it is forced to do so. [In 2005] the Security Council passed an unprecedented three resolutions against Sudan in one month. But these resolutions had little real consequence. For all the media attention, UN resolutions and diplomatic negotiations on Darfur, the international community is loath to commit to any action. Reeves noted that the Khartoum government sees this talk for what much of it is—empty threats.

Without a substantial UN or NATO [North Atlantic Treaty Organization] intervention, it will be extremely difficult for the ICC to build compelling cases against high-level officials in a timely manner. Many observers have noted that one of

Sudan's Attempts to Discredit the Court

The ongoing conflict and Khartoum's deliberate obstruction of the ICC's work make it difficult to inform Darfuris about the court, which has come under fire from NGOs [nongovernmental organizations] for the limited scale of its outreach work done in Sudan so far.

As the grave security situation forces ICC investigators to work from countries like Chad—where hundreds of thousands of displaced Darfuris have sought refuge in a number of camps—they have no physical presence in Darfur or elsewhere in Sudan.

One person [the Institute of War & Peace Reporting, IWPR] spoke to said the ICC was "just a rumour, more or less".

An extensive government-sponsored disinformation campaign, plus censorship and self-censorship, are obstacles to the ICC spreading word of its work among Darfuris. Newpapers are not widely available and the stories that do exist are often one-sided.

A Sudanese journalist told IWPR that the government-controlled press publishes false information in order to discredit the court.

In the past, the authorities have sought to portray the ICC as some kind of conspiracy between the US and Israel—even though neither country has ratified the court. . . .

In this repressive climate, discussing the ICC is taboo and many are reluctant to do so, which made finding people who were comfortable to speak to IWPR quite a challenge. It also meant we had to be careful over who[m] we approached for views about the ICC, as we did not want to get anyone into trouble for associating with us.

Katy Glassborow et al., Sudan Tribune,
October 18, 2007.

the reasons the government has been resistant to UN involvement is fear that UN forces will be used to serve arrest warrants from the ICC.

Igniting More Violence

It is also possible that the ICC investigation has brought more violence to the conflict. Even before the ICC referral was announced, the government in Khartoum came out fighting. Military and government officials made repeated claims that war would start again if the ICC began to prosecute, some warning that it would become another Iraq. Agence France Press quoted Sudan President Omar Bashir as saying, "Thrice in the name of Almighty Allah . . . I shall never hand any Sudanese national to a foreign court." He warned that Darfur would become a "graveyard" for international forces.

A UN commission of inquiry on Darfur recommended the referral to the ICC and provided the ICC's prosecutor with a sealed list of fifty-one people accused of crimes against humanity and war crimes in Darfur. While the prosecutor is not bound to this much-discussed list of names, the specter of prosecution has clearly instilled fear in the Sudanese government in Khartoum. Reeves speculates that the list likely includes First Vice President Ali Osman Taha, Janjaweed and rebel officials, and very possibly President Omar Bashir. Many advocates of the ICC suggested that the fear of looming prosecution would act as a deterrent for the military and government officials in Sudan. Reeves, however, disagrees: "One of the most disingenuous moments in the ICC referral was the notion that this might have a deterrence. This will not have a deterrent effect. It will make the regime more aggressive."

A marked government has little to lose. [In 2005], Kofi Annan admitted to the UN General Assembly, "The possibility cannot be excluded that those who may believe that they are on the commission's sealed list of war crimes suspects will resort to direct attacks against ... international personnel, or will try to destabilize the region more generally through violence."

Khartoum's violent threats are the reflexes of a government that is clearly cornered. No one has suggested that the ICC is not right for the situation; it is simply a lot to ask an untested court to accomplish alone and quickly. Even with the progress made, the government may be allowed to stay safely in that corner for quite some time. Indeed, it has done so for years. "It's not a question of what should be done. It's a question of how many will die. We know we need force; 7,000 are dying every month and will continue to die," Reeves observed.

"After the ICC referral, there was a weakening of political resolve in the Security Council and among member countries. This is very problematic," Deirdre Clancy said in a phone interview.

The World Is Losing Faith

Meanwhile, those in Darfur wonder what has happened to The Hague. "The victims who must flee their homes only to see their wives and daughters raped and their husbands and sons shot favor the use of the International Criminal Court," said Refugees International worker Mamie Mutchler after visiting Darfur. "It seems only fair that their voices should weigh heavily in this debate." NGOs [nongovernmental organizations] and human rights organizations in Sudan have suggested that the public is losing faith in the ICC, as they can't see any progress.

International officials are already starting to get restless. Louise Arbour, the UN High Commissioner for Human Rights, recently called upon the ICC "to more robustly and visibly discharge its mandate and the referral by the Security Council." But the ICC cannot fulfill its mandate with visibility, when any visibility at all is a security risk for witnesses, ICC staff and possibly the whole region. Sudan's minister of justice explained the sense of insecurity: "Many difficulties hold back efforts to track the criminals. . . . Even the witnesses run for their lives."

This is the context for the ICC's first cases. While the UN assembles a peacekeeping mission that is unlikely to have the mandate or numbers to be successful in Sudan, and as the United States and NATO continue to drag their feet, the ICC investigation slowly moves on, struggling to bring a measure of justice to areas the rest of the world won't touch.

| "U.S. diplomatic half-steps in Congo undermine our long-term strategic goals in Africa."

The United States Should Commit to Ending War in the Congo

Mvemba Phezo Dizolele

Mvemba Phezo Dizolele is an independent journalist based in Washington, DC. He spent the summer of 2006 traveling through the Democratic Republic of the Congo reporting on the conflict there. In the following viewpoint, Dizolele argues that waffling U.S. policy toward the war in Congo is exacerbating the conflict. He states that the lack of commitment to ending the war is emboldening the warlords in the country and their supporters from neighboring Rwanda and Uganda. Dizolele recommends that the United States should work with the United Nations to halt the supply of arms and munitions from Rwanda and Uganda, support the prosecution of war criminals, and provide money and personnel to assist in the training of the Congolese military and police units to fight the warring militias.

As you read, consider the following questions:

1. According to Dizolele, about how many Congolese die every month in that country's conflict?
2. In Dizolele's report, what are the militias fighting for?
3. Given the lack of U.S. assistance, what nations are shouldering the responsibility of aiding Congo's security sector, according to the author?

When Nelson Mandela was released from jail in 1990 and during the subsequent 1994 independence and elections in South Africa, the United States displayed a dramatic commitment to the democratic movement in Africa that has not been in evidence since. That seemed to change, however, with the U.S.-sanctioned arrest of Liberia's former president, Charles Taylor, on March 29, 2006, for human rights violations in neighboring Sierra Leone.

The United States, which helped broker the 2003 political arrangement that offered Taylor safe haven in Nigeria and shielded him from prosecution, reversed its position and demanded his extradition to Sierra Leone. In a rare departure, the United States held itself and its African allies, such as Nigeria's Olusegun Obasanjo and Liberia's Ellen Johnson-Sirleaf, to Jeffersonian standards and ideals of justice and freedom.

Africans have fought for the respect of human rights for the past 50 years with limited success. [Since 1985], however, they have instigated several initiatives to end impunity, including special tribunals in Ethiopia, the International Criminal Tribunal for Rwanda (Arusha), attempts to prosecute Chad's former president, Hissen Habré, and Truth and Reconciliation Commissions in South Africa, Ghana, and Sierra Leone. With the exception of the International Criminal Tribunal for Rwanda and the Sudan peace accord, which benefited from American activism, the United States has shown little enthusiasm or support for these initiatives.

Taylor's arrest promises a new level of commitment to justice in U.S. policy toward Africa, one defined by the advancement of self-evident and inalienable rights. In the post-9/11 world, such a policy would yield better results than any billion-dollar public relations campaign the State Department could wage to win the hearts and minds of the oppressed.

Warring Factions

Now, President [George W.] Bush, Secretary of State [Condoleeza] Rice, and Congress should muster the same political will and exert true pressure on Rwanda's Paul Kagame and Uganda's Yoweri Museveni to end the conflict in Congo, Africa's deadliest since World War II. Rwanda and Uganda are the primary sponsors of the militias destabilizing eastern Congo. The conflict, which began in 1998, has claimed more than 4.4 million victims. On average more than 31,000 people die every month, 45 percent of them children under the age of five. Unless we act forcefully, Congo has no future.

In the spirit of the peace accord signed between the rebel groups and President Joseph Kabila in 2003 in Sun City, South Africa, Congo held its first multiparty elections in more than four decades on July 30, 2006. The accord, which both Rwanda and Uganda supported, called for all armed factions to be integrated into a unified national army before the elections. The two countries had previously signed separate agreements with Congo in 2002 to withdraw their troops from Congolese territory.

[In 2006], however, as the Congolese await election results, the unification of the armed factions has yet to materialize. Even though they wear the same army uniform, these militias maintain parallel structures and commands, often disregarding instructions from the general headquarters in Kinshasa. They pledge allegiance and loyalty to, and take their orders directly from, their leaders in the transitional government. In several instances, units have fought against each other. Congo's corrupt transitional government finds itself with an unpaid, undertrained, underequipped, and disorganized army with a weak central command. Without an army, the government can neither protect its citizens nor defend Congo's territorial integrity.

This situation reflects the greatest weakness of the Sun City Accord, which offered carrots to the signatories but brandished no sticks at the belligerents. Most of the positions in the transitional government went either to former fighters, including the Kabila camp, or their proxies. Overnight, the warlords became government officials, with full immunity but no popular mandate.

Many of these leaders are guilty of war crimes, gross human rights violations, and corruption. Yet only one warlord, Thomas Lubanga, has been indicted [in August 2006] by the International Criminal Court for human rights abuses and the conscription of child soldiers. A new government may lead to the prosecution of these leaders, an outcome they do not welcome. With little chance to win in the elections, these former warlords have no incentive to give up their militias. Neither are they interested in a successful transition. Unless they are prosecuted (or threatened with prosecution) after the elections, those warlords would resume the conflict in an effort to remain in the political system and enjoy immunity from legal action. The same applies to their sponsors in Rwanda and Uganda.

The U.N. Is Failing to Keep the Peace

With 17,000 troops and a $1 billion yearly budget, the United Nations Mission in Congo (MONUC) runs the world's most expensive peacekeeping operation. Yet in parts of the country where rape and violence are the daily lot of helpless civilians, the mission has, in fact, become the symbol of impunity. U.N. troops and their civilian leaders often lack the will to apply their mandate, which is to use force against militias to protect civilians.

In recent months, the peacekeepers have stepped up their efforts to apply that mandate in certain parts of the country, particularly in Ituri province, where U.N. troops have been battling militias alongside the Congolese national army. This is the level of commitment that is required for peace to take hold in Congo.

MONUC's budget is too high for a mission that has done little to restore long-term stability and security in the region. But even if MONUC were not wasteful and unsuccessful, a U.N. peacekeeping mission is not a good long-term replacement for a competent and professional national army.

The United States is the largest contributor to MONUC's budget, and William Swing, the head of the U.N. peacekeeping mission in Congo, is an American. Yet the United States supports the Rwandan and Ugandan governments, primary sponsors of the militias that undermine MONUC's performance. In the end, U.S. taxpayers fund a U.N. mission that their own government policies undercut through inconsistent diplomacy.

Despite its checkered performance, MONUC has been an important deterrent to the escalation of conflict. As MONUC's largest contributor, the United States should demand better performance and greater accountability and exert more pressure on the mission to enforce its mandate until Congo can raise and train a professional and competent army and police force. The U.N. Security Council should extend MONUC's term and expand its capabilities for that purpose.

Establishing Law and Order

The Congolese have witnessed unspeakable crimes and unimaginable atrocities. The architects of and participants in the war must be held accountable. Congo alone does not have the resources to establish a tribunal to address the crimes. As with Rwanda and Sierra Leone, the transition to democracy requires establishing and maintaining a sense of justice among the people. A tribunal would facilitate reconciliation not only

Central African Countries

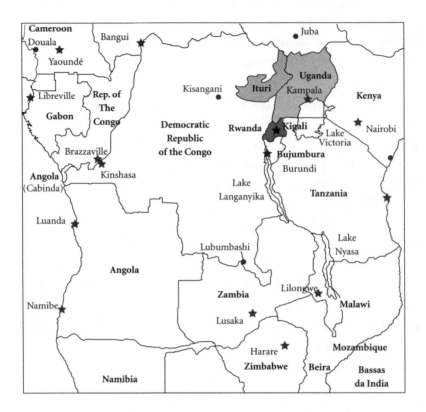

in Congo but in the [African] Great Lakes region as a whole. As history has shown, impunity only fuels hatred and instability. Without a tribunal, the survivors will take justice into their own hands and the conflict will never end.

The lack of a unified army and police force is the primary conflict driver. The security vacuum has created the right conditions for the continuation of the war, especially in the postelection period because some former rebel leaders will no longer have access to power or immunity from prosecution.

The struggle for control over natural resources and mineral wealth is at the core of the conflict. Groups with access to mineral-rich areas generate large sums of revenue through illegal exploitation and trade of resources, and they have no interest in the return of law and order. The 2003 U.N. Panel of Experts on the Illegal Exploitation of Natural Resources accused both Rwanda and Uganda of prolonging the civil war so that they could siphon off Congo's wealth with the help of Western corporations.

Ironically, Rwanda and Uganda, the two neighbors that would most benefit from peace in Congo, continue to fuel the conflict through their logistic support of militias. This support comes in the form of arms transfers, financial assistance, military advising, military training, and safe harbor to those who flee the Congolese national government. These actions violate the U.N. embargo on the flow of arms into Congo. With this proliferation of arms, the already crippled Congolese government is unable to secure its borders, and both Rwanda and Uganda have used border insecurity as a pretext to invade Congo.

A Consistent U.S. Policy

U.S. Congo policy has been ambivalent at best and incongruent and inconsistent at worst.

To avert a civil war following the elections, the United States should display the same drive and determination, including exerting pressure on those financing and enabling the conflict, as it did to accomplish Charles Taylor's extradition to Sierra Leone. The Congo crisis provides Congress another opportunity to show U.S. commitment to democratic values, advancement of human rights, and the promotion of the rule of law in Africa. The pervasive climate of impunity, local and international, is the greatest threat to peace and security in Congo.

Inconsistent U.S. diplomacy helps fuel the conflict. War criminals should be prosecuted without prejudice. President Bush and Congress should hold Rwanda and Uganda responsible for their actions and exert the appropriate pressure to uphold the U.N. arms embargo, which means prosecuting violators. The United States has failed to join multidonor efforts to restore justice in Congo's Ituri and eastern provinces. Most important, the United States has failed to follow up on its *own* justice initiative after Ambassador-at-Large for War Crimes Issues Pierre-Richard Prosper commissioned a Woodrow Wilson School of Public and International Affairs assessment of justice and impunity in the Great Lakes region.

In 2005, the International Court of Justice fined Uganda $10 billion for looting Congo's natural resources and human rights abuses perpetrated by Ugandan troops on Congolese civilians. Whether Uganda pays the fine or not, Ugandan officers responsible for the atrocities should be prosecuted.

Furthermore, the United States should fully support the recommendations of the U.N. Panel of Experts on the Illegal Exploitation of Natural Resources and help prosecute those individuals and corporations mentioned in the report. To date, U.S. inaction has benefited the perpetrators and by default fueled the conflict. In fact, failure to act on the panel's recommendations has sent the message to corrupt Congolese government officials that the United States will tolerate business as usual in the extractive industries. In contrast, the United Kingdom, through diplomatic channels, has promoted the Extractive Industry Transparency Initiative, whose positive signal has been well received among anticorruption activists in Africa. Congo's resources should be sold by means of a transparent global bidding system that would benefit the Congolese people and interested corporations. The country needs these resources to rebuild its economy.

U.S. Help to Bolster Congo's Security

As for the establishment, integration, and training of the national army and police, Congo needs more partners with bigger resources and expertise for the daunting task ahead. Without a robust army and law enforcement structures, Congo will have no peace after the elections. Yet the United States contributes next to nothing to security-sector reform in Congo, leaving it to Angola, South Africa, Belgium, France, and the World Bank to shoulder that responsibility. The United States should send money, send military and police instructors (some of whom could be private contractors), and exert greater pressure on leaders in Kinshasa to integrate their militias by allowing the international community to take over security-sector reform. A U.S. presence could solve the lack of coordination among and between donors and the Congolese army factions.

Congo's extraordinary circumstances require bold measures. Unless the United States reconsiders its Congo policy and deals vigorously with the negative forces, including Rwandan and Ugandan influences, the conflict is likely to escalate beyond its current cataclysmic proportions. The stakes are high: U.S. diplomatic half-steps in Congo undermine our long-term strategic goals in Africa. We should either fully commit to help the Congolese solve the conflict or not commit at all.

As he did for the Sudan, President Bush should appoint a special envoy for Congo to help coordinate the administration's efforts and articulate its position. In addition, Congress should set up a task force to review the current Congo policy, or lack thereof, and realign U.S. diplomacy in Central Africa with our long-term strategic goals. In its campaign against global terror, the United States cannot afford to waste the goodwill that Charles Taylor's indictment has generated among Africans. The United States should build on that momentum and win Congo, the very heart of Africa.

| *"Congress should legislate a moratorium*
| *on arms sales to all regions of conflict."*

The United States Should Stop Selling Arms to Africa

Rachel Stohl

The following viewpoint is the text of a speech that Rachel Stohl delivered to the U.S. Congressional Human Rights Caucus. In the viewpoint, Stohl describes how small arms and light weapons have contributed to millions of deaths in West Africa. Stohl praises various international agreements that would limit or ban weapons sales to the region, but she maintains that the United States is a key factor in making such treaties work and must take a stronger hand in stopping the proliferation of small arms. Stohl argues that Congress must legislate a ban on U.S. weapons sales to the continent and should help African nations destroy stockpiles of small arms already in existence. Rachel Stohl is a senior analyst at the Center for Defense Information, a research institute that focuses on U.S. security and defense policy.

As you read, consider the following questions:

1. As Stohl states, what have weapons been commonly traded for in Sierra Leone and Liberia?

Rachel Stohl, "The Legacy of Illicit Small Arms: Devastation in West Africa," Center for Defense Information, May 20, 2004. Reproduced by permission.

2. Why should the United States be concerned about small arms proliferation in West Africa, according to Stohl?

3. What three things does the author suggest the U.S. government should do to address the proliferation of small arms in Africa?

I am pleased to be here today to talk to you about an issue that has for years been overshadowed by other crucial foreign policy discussions. The need to address small arms today is urgent and critical. The human cost of small arms proliferation is immeasurable. Small arms are a class of weapons responsible for an estimated 500,000 deaths and thousands more injuries each year. Women and children suffer disproportionately from the proliferation of small arms. The spread and misuse of small arms cause, prolong, and exacerbate humanitarian crises around the world. Today we are focusing on one particular region—West Africa—where the devastating effects of small arms are all too clear.

In this brief presentation, I want to give you an overview of the SALW [small arms, light weapons] problem in West Africa, steps the region, continent, and international community are taking to mitigate the problems caused by SALW proliferation and misuse, and specific policies the United States can undertake to assist in reducing the negative consequences of SALW in West Africa.

Cheap, Available Weapons

The number of small arms in West Africa is estimated at 7–8 million, with a minimum of 77,000 in the hands of West African insurgent groups. For example, Guinea Bissau, one of the poorest countries in the world, is estimated to have 25,000 weapons in circulation, and Nigeria is believed to have at least 1 million illicit small arms. These weapons are not necessarily new to the region, as recirculation of weapons—stockpiles left over from the Cold War when Africa was a cold battleground—have left a dramatic legacy on the people and countries of West Africa. However, new weapons supplies have entered West Africa from former Soviet States in recent years as well. Weapons are not only easily available, they can also be purchased cheaply. One recent report found that in Nigeria one could acquire pistols for between \$25–\$58, depending on the type. During the conflicts in Sierra Leone and Liberia, guns were commonly traded for diamonds and other resources. At this point, I would like to mention that we should not underestimate the role that diamonds have played in the proliferation of arms in West Africa. Diamonds, and other commodities, such as timber, have fueled the West African arms trade and allowed conflicts to perpetuate for decades. Arms brokering has become a lucrative trade in West Africa. Currently, the United Nations is investigating arms trafficking to and through Liberia during the regime of Charles Taylor.

Throughout West Africa, small arms are in the hands of states and non-state actors, meaning ethnic militia groups, private security companies, arms smugglers, criminal gangs, bandits, mercenaries, and vigilantes. These groups often act with impunity, using small arms to wage wars, terrorize civilian populations, and commit horrific human rights abuses. Experts estimate that 2 million West Africans alone have died in conflicts involving SALW since 1990. Moreover, the Coalition to Stop the Use of Child Soldiers believes that more than 120,000 African children under the age of 18 are used as soldiers in conflicts perpetuated by the availability and use of small arms.

Weapons Treaties

[Since 1999], states have given greater recognition to the devastating consequences of small arms. Africa has become home to continental and regional efforts to control SALW proliferation—both through legal and illicit channels. West Africa houses the UN Regional Centre for Peace and Disarmament in Africa located in Lome, Togo. And, West Africa was subjected to two arms embargoes in the 1990s—as both Sierra Leone and Liberia were put under UN arms embargoes in 1997 and 1992 respectively. But, there have also been concrete regional and international steps to control small arms that have an impact on proliferation in West Africa. I want to mention four of these briefly.

The first is the ECOWAS Moratorium—on Importation, Exportation, and Manufacture of Light Weapons. The Moratorium was initially signed October 31, 1998 for a 3 year period. It was extended for an additional 3 years July 5, 2001 and is valid until October 31, 2004. [It was not renewed thereafter.] The 16 ECOWAS member states—Benin, Burkina Faso, Cape Verde, Cote d'Ivoire, The Gambia, Ghana, Guinea, Guinea-Bissau, Liberia, Mali, Mauritania, Niger, Nigeria, Senegal, Sierra Leone, and Togo—adopted the moratorium because of the realization that small arms and light weapons have been the primary weapons involved in the multitude of conflicts that have plagued West Africa in the past decade, most notably in Liberia, Sierra Leone, Ivory Coast, and Guinea Bissau. The Moratorium allows for states to apply for exemptions to meet national security needs or international peacekeeping requirements, but otherwise is intended as a true moratorium. The regime has 3 parts—the moratorium itself, the Plan of Action for PCASED, the Program of Coordination and Assistance on Security and Development that acts as the supporting mechanism and secretariat for the moratorium, and Code of Conduct, which sets out the details of the Moratorium. The moratorium itself is not binding.

Second, in preparation for the 2001 UN Conference, African States adopted the Bamako Declaration December 1, 2000 in order to develop a common African approach to SALW and to ensure codification, harmonization, and standardization of national norms and the enhancement of sub-regional and continental cooperation among police, customs, and border control services. The Declaration encourages:

- Creation of national coordination agencies for small arms

- Enhancement of the capacity of national law enforcement and security agencies and officials, including training and upgrading of equipment and resources

- Destruction of surplus and confiscated weapons

- Development of public awareness programs

- Conclusion of bilateral arrangements for small arms control in common frontier zones

Third is the UN Protocol Against the Illicit Manufacture of and Trafficking in Firearms, Their Parts and Components and Ammunition—adopted by the General Assembly on May 31, 2001. The Protocol:

- Promotes uniform international standards for the international movement of firearms of import, export and transit

- Fosters cooperation and exchange of information at national, regional, and global levels, including firearms identification, detecting and tracing; and

- Promotes international firearms cooperation through the development of an international system to manage commercial shipments.

To date, only one-third of ECOWAS states are signatories to the Protocol—Benin, Burkina Faso, Mali, Nigeria, Senegal, Sierra Leone—and only Burkina Faso and Mali have ratified the Protocol.

Fourth is the UN Programme of Action [PoA], which arose from the 2001 UN Conference, on the Illicit Trade of Small Arms and Light Weapons in all its aspects. The Programme of

Action is a politically binding document with recommendations for states at the national, regional, and global levels to stop the illicit proliferation of SALW. For example, the PoA calls for:

- The establishment of a national focal point and coordination agency on small arms

- Disarmament, Demobilization & Re-integration (DDR) of ex-combatants, including collection and destruction of their weapons

- Better enforcement of arms embargoes

- More complete information exchanges

- Inclusion of civil society organizations in efforts to prevent SALW proliferation

Only 7 of the ECOWAS states submitted reports on their implementation of the PoA (Benin, Burkina Faso, Cote d'Ivoire, The Gambia, Mali, Niger, and Senegal) in 2003. And, only 5 West African Countries have established National Points of Contact (Burkina Faso, Ivory Coast, The Gambia, Guinea, Senegal). While State action on the PoA has been spotty in West Africa, civil society, particularly the West African Action Network on Small Arms (WAANSA), has been incredibly helpful in coordinating civil society organizations and working with governments in their efforts to stop the proliferation of small arms and to work to implement the PoA at the regional level.

Impact on U.S. Involvement in West Africa

I want to end by stating that the dangers of small arms go beyond the borders of West Africa and are a genuine threat to U.S. national interests and security. Small arms proliferation in one region can lead to proliferation in another. These weapons perpetuate violent conflict and create new cycles of violence and crime. Often, these conflicts require U.S. and international involvement, which puts U.S. troops and peacekeepers at risk as they are often the targets of small arms violence. At the end of 2003 U.S. Marines deployed in Liberia were threatened by small arms and efforts to disarm warring factions were hindered due to the massive number of weapons in circulation. On an economic front, small arms proliferation diminishes U.S. business opportunities abroad and raises the costs of doing business. From the humanitarian side, small arms proliferation undermines the ability of humanitarian and relief organizations to conduct their efforts, and weakens the possibilities for sustainable development.

Thwarting Terrorism by Arms Control

Controlling the flow of small arms is an integral part of the efforts underway to fight terrorism. Terrorist networks will continue to thrive if the root causes of their actions are not addressed, and if the flow of the tools of their trade are not hindered. From disarming ex-combatants and destroying surplus stockpiles of weapons to prevent their theft or diversion, to maintaining strict criteria for small arms exports and incorporating strict end-use monitoring, controlling the proliferation of small arms is essential to prevent these deadliest of weapons from ending up in the hand of terrorists. The porous borders in West Africa have allowed the Algerian terrorist group Salafist Group for Call and Combat (GSPC) to operate within the region. While West Africa is not the origin of well-established terrorist networks, the stockpiles of small arms available in the region are attractive to terrorist groups hunting for cheap, easily available weapons to conduct their activities.

Ban Arms Sales to Africa

The United States must support the existing regional and international efforts to control the proliferation and misuse of small arms. Through both financial and diplomatic means, the

Mozambique Works to Disarm Itself

The Mozambican gun collection program is unique in many ways. It is sponsored by the Christian Council of Mozambique, or CCM, an umbrella group of 24 local churches.

When villagers find a weapons cache or someone just wants to get rid of an individual gun, they notify the CCM. A team comes to destroy or disable the weapons on the spot. Then, if any gun parts are left, they are turned over to the artists to shape into sculptures, which sell for hundreds of dollars.

In exchange for the weapons, the villagers get tools or other goods to help improve their lives. Sometimes, they get sewing machines, sometimes bicycles.

Challis McDonough, Voice of America,
December 29, 2004.

United States must provide resources and expertise to implement provisions of the ECOWAS Moratorium, the Bamako declaration, the UN Protocol and UN PoA. U.S. leadership on the small arms issue, from encouraging West African States to meet their regional and international obligations to ensuring that U.S. weapons aren't transferred to the region are key steps in halting the dire effects of small arms in the West African region. There are also institutional steps the United States can take to ensure that small arms are addressed.

First, Congress should legislate a moratorium on arms sales to all regions of conflict—especially ongoing conflicts—a policy that was announced by former Secretary of State Madeleine Albright in 1999, but was never addressed by Congress. West Africa will continue to see conflict until there is a widespread commitment to ensure new stocks do not enter the supply chain.

Destroy Stockpiles and Limit Proliferation

Second, not only should new supplies of small arms be halted, but existing stockpiles must be mopped up. West African countries would benefit from community-based weapons-collection programs. Rather than turning in weapons for cash, a neighborhood could receive increased security patrols, assistance with rebuilding schools, roads, shops, or provision of electricity, for a target number of weapons turned in. AK-47s, rocket propelled grenades, and missiles have no place in households. Once weapons are collected, the United States has two choices: to assist with their destruction or to ensure that the weapons are suitably secured. Destruction need not be a costly or burdensome endeavour. The United States has experience training local populations on weapons destruction, and has recently provided technical and financial assistance to destruction programs in 10 countries at a total cost of only $5.25 million, destroying nearly 300,000 weapons and over 7.5 million rounds of ammunition. Because known arms depots are often poorly guarded, and have become reliable sources for those individuals seeking weapons, the United States must begin training West Africans in proper stockpile security and management. Indeed the United States already has such model programs underway in several other countries.

Third, the United States should support the development of legally binding norms and the implementation of measures to stop weapons from winding up in the hands of abusive forces, be they either governments or non-state actors. In general, the United States should look to export its best practices in addressing the proliferation of small arms and assist those governments that do not have adequate export controls in place to develop reliable systems. The United States already has one of the best export control systems in the world and should look to internationalize our best practices. This includes assisting West African countries in developing national and international regulations on arms brokering and the strict adherence to arms embargoes.

These are just some of the steps the United States can take, all of which will lead to progress on the issue. Action on small arms is a step-by-step process requiring a long-term effort. But in the short term, U.S. action and leadership on small arms will begin the process of undoing the damage these weapons cause. While immediate and future action on small arms in West Africa should include partnership between governments and NGOs [nongovernmental organizations], in the end, it is governments, those within West Africa and those that have the capacity to help, that must be held accountable. The bottom line is that addressing small arms is about saving lives, ending human suffering, and creating a more sustainable and peaceful future.

Periodical Bibliography

The following articles have been selected to supplement the diverse views presented in this chapter.

Greg Collins	"Incorporating Africa's Conflicts into the War on Terror," *Peace Review*, July–September 2007.
Helene Cooper	"A Story in Which Only the Happy Ending Is Unusual," *New York Times*, April 2, 2006.
Sally B. Donnelly	"A Command for Africa," *Time*, September 4, 2006.
Economist	"Africa Acknowledges It Must Help Itself," July 9, 2005.
Danny Glover and Nicole C. Lee	"Say No to Africom," *Nation*, November 19, 2007.
Eric Hoskins	"Africa's Endless War," *Maclean's*, May 17, 2004.
Nicholas D. Kristof	"Africa's World War," *New York Times*, June 14, 2007.
John Lasker	"Genocide Not Enough to Send in Troops?" *Black Enterprise*, October 2006.
Abraham McLaughlin and Duncan Woodside	"Urgent Push on Africa's Oldest Civil War," *Christian Science Monitor*, November 17, 2004.
John Prendergast and Colin Thomas-Jensen	"Blowing the Horn," *Foreign Affairs*, March–April 2007.
Time	"Who Will Stop the Killing?" August 4, 2003.
Alex de Waal	"The Wars of Sudan," *Nation*, March 19, 2007.
Jeremy M. Weinstein	"Africa's Revolutionary Deficit," *Foreign Policy*, July/August 2007.
Kevin Whitelaw	"The Mutating Threat," *U.S. News and World Report*, December 26, 2005.

For Further Discussion

Chapter 1

1. A large number of organizations, including government agencies, have testified to the problem of AIDS in sub-Saharan African countries. How does Tom Bethell deflate the crisis, insisting that the "epidemic" has been exaggerated by political opportunists? Do you believe Bethell's assertions? Explain why or why not.

2. After reading the viewpoints in this chapter, explain what you believe is the most pressing problem in Africa. Clearly defend why this problem, above all others, needs to be addressed first. Then explain how remedying this problem will lead to the betterment of Africa and possibly the eradication of the other less-important problems.

3. In her viewpoint, Tina Butler argues that Africa is unfairly suffering from the supposed calamity of global warming despite the fact that "Africa emits far less carbon than other continents." Looking at the host of problems addressed in this chapter, how much responsibility does Africa bear for the crisis posed by each one? If Africa is not wholly or even partially to blame, in your opinion, who is responsible for these problems? Explain your answer.

Chapter 2

1. Andrew Mwenda argues that foreign aid money is not helping Africa in part because it subsidizes corrupt governments and does not force these governments to curb their illicit practices and make needed economic reforms. Jeffrey Sachs maintains that other forms of aid—such as the building of schools and the improvement of health—are benefiting African nations even if corruption is inter-

fering with financial assistance. If you were in charge of a large aid package (that included monetary and other types of assistance) to an African nation, explain how you would maximize the benefits while minimizing the potential for graft? Would you place conditions on the recipient nation? Why or why not?

2. Of debt relief, free trade, foreign investment, and foreign aid, which economic incentive do you think is most needed in Africa? Citing from the viewpoints, explain how this incentive would have the most beneficial impact on African economies.

Chapter 3

1. Sebastien Arnold makes the case that Western democracy may be a poor fit for Africa, especially because it seems to be benefiting a select elite and not the vast majority of Africans who do not quite understand its principles or implementation. This may be, he says, because Western democracy ignores the cultural norms that shape African society. Jerry Rawlings, the former president of Ghana, supports Arnold's view that African governments are likely to do better with democracy if they dispense with the Western model and build upon African traditions. After considering the evidence Arnold and Rawlings present, explain whether you think democracy can succeed—or is succeeding— in Africa. You may use the arguments of Jennifer Widner in framing your response.

2. Deputy secretary-general of the United Nations Asha-Rose Migiro provides several examples of sub-Saharan African nations that are improving their human rights records. She states that the media is to blame for ignoring these successes and instead portraying Africa as a continent plagued by human rights abuses. After reading the human

rights report of Amnesty International, do you think Migiro's finger-pointing is justified? Explain why or why not.

3. After reading all the viewpoints in this chapter, do you think that democratic reform should precede economic reform in African nations? Explain why or why not.

Chapter 4

1. What arguments does Anja Tranovich use to question the power and reach of the International Criminal Court (ICC)? Do you think these criticisms are valid? Why or why not? Do some outside reading on the ICC and its previous record of war-crimes trials. Do you believe the ICC can bring justice to Darfur, Sudan? Explain your answer.

2. Consider the opinions expressed in this chapter. Then answer the tough foreign policy question, "Is America doing enough to promote peace in Africa?" In creating your response be sure to think about America's other global commitments as well as what interests America has in facilitating peace in Africa.

Organizations to Contact

The editors have compiled the following list of organizations concerned with the issues debated in this book. The descriptions are derived from materials provided by the organizations. All have publications or information available for interested readers. The list was compiled on the date of publication of the present volume; the information provided here may change. Be aware that many organizations take several weeks or longer to respond to inquiries, so allow as much time as possible.

Africa Action
1634 Eye St. NW, #810, Washington, DC   20006
(202) 546-7961 • fax: (202) 546-1545
e-mail: africaaction@igc.org
Web site: www.africaaction.org

Africa Action is a national organization promoting U.S. government policy that aids in the achievement of peace and development in Africa. Through education and public awareness programs, the organization seeks to ensure fair treatment and equal opportunity for those living in Africa. Africa Action publishes the annual report *Africa Policy Outlook*, and offers other reports such as *Africa Action on Darfur, Africa Action on HIV/AIDS*, and *Africa Action on Debt* on its Web site.

African Union (AU)
PO Box 3243, Addis Ababa
   Ethiopia
(251) 11-551-77-00 • fax: (251) 11-551-78-44
Web site: www.africa-union.org

Established in 1999 as the Organization of African Unity, the AU provides a central organizing body to address the continent's most pressing problems. Over time, the work of the AU has focused on issues such as the effects of post-colonization and apartheid, increasing development, and uni-

198

fication of African countries while still observing national sovereignty. The union has published reports on significant continental events such as the genocide in Rwanda (*Rwanda: The Preventable Genocide*) as well as the conflict in Sierra Leone (*The Sierra Leone Truth & Reconciliation Report*).

AVERT

4 Brighton Rd., West Sussex   RF13 5BA
  UK
e-mail: info@avert.org
Web site: www.avert.org

The international AIDS charity AVERT works to reduce the number and impact of HIV/AIDS infections globally through education and promotion of positive, proactive treatment of the disease. Many of the organization's projects focus on Africa and India, with an emphasis on prevention as well as aid for those already impacted by AIDS. AVERT's Web site offers regional summaries of the AIDS epidemic as well as more detailed, specific reports about the prevalence of the disease within particular countries such as South Africa, Malawi, and Uganda.

Climate Institute

1785 Massachusetts Ave. NW, Washington, DC   20036
(202) 547-0104 • fax: (202) 547-0111
e-mail: info@climate.org
Web site: www.climate.org

A nonprofit organization dedicated to educating and influencing the decisions of policy makers worldwide, the Climate Institute employs the expertise of individuals around the globe and provides forums for the exchange of information and ideas about how to combat global climate change. The institute operates the Web site Climate.org to provide specific information about the effects of climate change such as sea level rise, extreme weather, ecosystems, and agriculture. *Climate*

Alert is the quarterly newsletter of the organization, and Climate.org features many links to reports concerning the impact of climate change on Africa.

Cato Institute

1000 Massachusetts Ave. NW, Washington, DC   20001-5403
(202) 842-0200 • fax: (202) 842-3490
Web site: www.cato.org

The Cato Institute, a nonprofit, public policy research organization promoting the principles of libertarianism, analyzes all aspects of the U.S. government's domestic and foreign policy, offers recommendations to policy makers, and educates the public on current issues debated in the government. One project of the institute, the Center for Global Liberty and Prosperity, studies the problems faced by developing nations and promotes free-market solutions as the best option to combat these problems. The center publishes the annual report *Economic Freedom of the World* as well as the periodic newsletter *Economic Development Bulletin.*

Economic Commission for Africa (ECA)

PO Box 3001, Addis Ababa
   Ethiopia
(251) 11-551-7200 • fax: (251) 11-551-2233
e-mail: ecainfo@uneca.org
Web site: www.uneca.org

ECA is a regional agency of the United Nations focusing on economic and social development within Africa. The commission works in cooperation with the African Union to implement programs that benefit the individual countries of Africa as well as the continent as a whole. Additionally, ECA focuses on the specific needs of African countries, especially with regard to poverty, growth, and development, and gender issues. Publications of the ECA include the annual *Economic Report on Africa*, as well as *Governance for a Progressing Africa*, and *Striving for Good Governance in Africa.*

The Foundation for Democracy in Africa (FDA)

1612 K St. NW, Suite 1104, Washington, DC   20006
(202) 331-1333 • fax: (202) 331-8547
e-mail: info@democracy-africa.org
Web site: www.democracy-africa.org

FDA operates as a nongovernmental organization with consultative status in the United Nations Economic and Social Council. The foundation works to promote programs in Africa that operate on and proliferate the fundamental principles of democracy and free-market economics. Additionally, FDA seeks to help existing African democracies establish themselves within the global economy. The foundation's Web site offers archived issues of the *Africa Growth and Opportunity Act Civil Society Network Newsletter* and the *Western Hemisphere African Diaspora Network Newsletter*.

Human Rights Watch (HRW)

350 Fifth Ave., 34th Fl., New York, NY   10118-3299
(212) 290-4700 • fax: (212) 736-1300
e-mail: hrwnyc@hrw.org
Web site: www.hrw.org

HRW is an international organization dedicated to ensuring that the human rights of individuals worldwide are observed and protected. In order to achieve this protection, HRW investigates allegations of human rights abuses then works to hold violators, be it governments or individuals, accountable for their actions. The organization's Web site is arranged by continent, offering specific information on individual countries and issues. In the Africa section, numerous reports and press releases are available on topics such as conflicts and abuses in Somalia, Sudan, and the Democratic Republic of Congo.

Institute for Human Rights and Development in Africa (IHRDA)

Brusubi Layout 949, Coastal Highway, PO Box 1896
   The Gambia
(00220) 996-2280 • fax: (00220) 449-4178
e-mail: info@africaninstitute.org
Web site: www.africaninstitute.org

IHRDA is a nongovernmental, pan-African organization striving to increase awareness and accessibility of human rights protection in Africa in coordination with the African Union. The institute works to accomplish this goal through training programs for human rights activists, free legal aid, research, networking, and advocacy. IHRDA publishes the *Compilation of Decisions of the African Commission,* a book containing text of the decisions of the Assembly of Heads of States and Government of the African Union; other information detailing the African Regional System is available on the organization's Web site.

International Fund for Agricultural Development (IFAD)

1775 K St. NW, Suite 410, Washington, DC   20006-1502
(202) 331-9099 • fax: (202) 331-9366
Web site: www.ifad.org

IFAD is the United Nations agency focused on combating the effects of rural poverty in developing countries and aiding individuals in poverty in establishing sustainable lifestyles. The organization provides loans and grants to developing countries' governments with low interest rates and acts as an advocate for the rural impoverished within the international community. IFAD works to educate the public about the effects of poverty and the possible solutions with the publication of reports such as *Enabling the Rural Poor to Overcome Poverty, Polishing the Stone* (concerning gender equality in rural development), and *Climate Change;* in addition, the organization has created numerous, country-specific facts sheets.

International Monetary Fund (IMF)

700 Nineteenth St. NW, Washington, DC   20431
(202) 623-7300 • fax: (202) 623-6278
e-mail: publicaffairs@imf.org
Web site: www.imf.org

IMF works to foster international trade to benefit all countries and promote economic cooperation worldwide. The organization also offers financial loans to nations in order to aid these countries in developing their economies. IMF collects information on all 185 member countries, both developed and developing nations, and serves as a clearinghouse for current data and statistics regarding the economic standing of these countries. The fund provides numerous fact sheets, pamphlets, and brochures, all of which are available on its Web site.

The Partnership to Cut Hunger and Poverty in Africa

499 S. Capitol St., Suite 500B, Washington, DC   20003
(202) 479-4501 • fax: (202) 488-0590
e-mail: partnership@africanhunger.org
Web site: www.africanhunger.org

The Partnership to Cut Hunger and Poverty in Africa formed in 2000 as a coalition of Africans and Americans concerned about the impact and prevalence of poverty and famine in Africa. The organization emphasizes the importance of using aid from the West, in particular from the United States, as a tool for ending hunger in Africa. The partnership works to ensure that aid packages are utilized in beneficial initiatives, such as rural development, to provide lasting results of reduced poverty. Publications of the organization include *Now Is the Time: A Plan to Cut Hunger and Poverty in Africa, The Right Way to Aid Africa, and Beating Africa's Poverty by Investing in Africa's Infrastructure.*

Third World Network Africa (TWN Africa)

9 Ollenu St., East Legon, PO Box AN 19452
Accra-North Ghana

e-mail: webjournalist@twnafrica.org
Web site: www.twnafrica.org

TWN Africa works to ensure that the rights and needs of Africans are observed and protected on a global scale through research and advocacy efforts. The network focuses on the promotion of sustainable development practices as central to the growth and well-being of individuals in developing countries as well as the importance of equal access to global resources. TWN Africa publishes the bimonthly magazine *African Agenda and* provides previous issues of the monthly newsletter *African Trade Agenda.*

UNAIDS
Regional Advisor on HIV/AIDS Situation, Washington, DC
(202) 223-7610 • fax: (202) 223-7616
Web site: www.unaids.org

UNAIDS is the United Nations agency providing efforts to internationally combat the AIDS epidemic. The organization focuses its efforts on areas such as prevention, treatment, and care; populations most affected by the disease; the broader effects of the disease on communities; and general research into vaccines and preventative measures. UNAIDS has published numerous documents detailing all aspects of this global disease, with most reports in their extensive catalog available on the organization's Web site in portable document format (pdf).

The World Bank
1818 H St. NW, Washington, DC   20433
(202) 473-1000 • fax: (202) 477-6391
e-mail: pic@worldbank.org
Web site: www.worldbank.org

The World Bank provides monetary assistance to developing countries worldwide in the form of low-interest loans. The money provided is intended to aid these countries in developing their economies and social and political infrastructures in order to reduce poverty on a global level. World Bank money in Africa had aided in the creation of schools and housing, as well as providing the basis for sustainable development and the reduction of HIV/AIDS. Current publications detailing the bank's activities in Africa include the book *Making Finance Work for Africa* and the studies *Facing the Challenges of African Growth: Opportunities, Constraints, and Strategic Directions* and *Africa Development Indicators 2006.*

Bibliography of Books

Taisier M. Ali and Robert O. Matthews, eds. — *Civil Wars in Africa: Roots and Resolution.* Montreal: McGill-Queen's University Press, 1999.

Jean-Paul Azam — *Trade, Exchange Rate, and Growth in Sub-Saharan Africa.* New York: Cambridge University Press, 2007.

Elias K. Bongmba — *Facing a Pandemic: The African Church and the Crisis of HIV/AIDS.* Waco, TX: Baylor University Press, 2007.

Jane Boulden, ed. — *Dealing with Conflict in Africa: The United Nations and Regional Organizations.* New York: Palgrave Macmillan, 2003.

Patrick Burnett and Firoze Manji, eds. — *From Slave Trade to Free Trade: How Trade Undermines Democracy and Justice in Africa.* Oxford, UK: Fahamu, 2007.

Robert Calderisi — *The Trouble with Africa: Why Foreign Aid Isn't Working.* New York: Palgrave Macmillan, 2006.

Catherine Campbell — *"Letting Them Die:" Why HIV/AIDS Prevention Programs Fail.* Bloomington: Indiana University Press, 2003.

Luc Christiaensen and Lionel Demery — *Down to Earth: Agriculture and Poverty Reduction in Africa.* Washington, DC: World Bank, 2007.

Paul Collier   *Breaking the Conflict Trap: Civil War and Development Policy.* Washington, DC: World Bank Publications, 2003.

Paul Collier and Nicholas Sambanis, eds.   *Understanding Civil War: Evidence and Analysis, Vol. 1: Africa.* Washington, DC: World Bank Publications, 2005.

Stephen Devereux and Simon Maxwell, eds.   *Food Security in Sub-Saharan Africa.* London: ITDG, 2001.

William Easterly   *The White Man's Burden: Why the West's Efforts to Aid the Rest Have Done So Much Ill and So Little Good.* New York: Penguin, 2006.

Helen Epstein   *The Invisible Cure: Africa, the West and the Fight Against AIDS.* New York: Farrar, Straus & Giroux: 2007.

James Ferguson   *Global Shadows: Africa in the Neoliberal World Order.* Durham, NC: Duke University Press, 2006.

Robert Guest   *The Shackled Continent: Africa's Past, Present and Future.* London: Macmillan, 2004.

Graham Hancock   *Lords of Poverty: The Power, Prestige, and Corruption of the International Aid Business.* New York: Atlantic Monthly Press, 1989.

Noreena Hertz   *The Debt Threat: How Debt Is Destroying the Developing World.* New York: HarperCollins, 2004.

Patrick Honohan and Thorsten Beck — *Making Finance Work for Africa.* Washington, DC: World Bank, 2007.

Susan Hunter — *Black Death: AIDS in Africa.* New York: Palgrave Macmillan, 2003.

George Klay Kieh Jr., ed. — *Beyond State Failure and Collapse: Making the State Relevant in Africa.* Lanham, MD: Lexington, 2007.

Staffan I. Lindberg — *Democracy and Elections in Africa.* Baltimore: Johns Hopkins University Press, 2006.

Michael Maren — *The Road to Hell: The Ravaging Effects of Foreign Aid and International Charity.* New York: Free Press, 1997.

Ama Mazama, ed. — *Africa in the 21st Century: Toward a New Future.* New York: Routledge, 2007.

John Mukum Mbaku — *Corruption in Africa: Causes, Consequences, and Cleanups.* Lanham, MD: Lexington, 2007.

Martin Meredith — *The Fate of Africa: A History of 50 Years of Independence.* New York: Public Affairs, 2005.

Muna Ndulo — *Democratic Reform in Africa: The Impact on Governance and Poverty Alleviation.* Athens: Ohio University Press, 2006.

Paul Nugent — *Africa Since Independence: A Comparative History.* New York: Palgrave Macmillan, 2004.

Obiora Chinedu Okafor — *The African Human Rights System, Activist Forces and International Institutions.* New York: Cambridge University Press, 2007.

Abdulahi A. Osman — *Governance and Internal Wars in Sub-Saharan Africa: Exploring the Relationship.* London: Adonis & Abbey, 2007.

Maano Ramutsindela — *Transfrontier Conservation in Africa: At the Confluence of Capital, Politics, and Nature.* Cambridge, MA: CABI, 2007.

Jeffrey D. Sachs — *The End of Poverty: Economic Possibilities for Our Time.* New York: Penguin, 2005.

Peter Schwab — *Africa: A Continent Self-Destructs.* New York: Palgrave, 2001.

Anne Seidman, Robert B. Seidman, Pumzo Mbana, and Hanson Hu Li, eds. — *Africa's Challenge: Using Law for Good Governance and Development.* Trenton, NJ: Africa World Press, 2007.

Joseph E. Siglitz and Andrew Charlton — *Fair Trade for All: How Trade Can Promote Development.* New York: Oxford University Press, 2005.

I. William Zartman — *Ripe for Resolution: Conflict and Intervention in Africa.* New York: Oxford University Press, 1985.

Index